Palliare

Palliare

Hard Edges and the Holy at the Edge of Life

Marci Pounders

Illustrated by Arthur Howard Orr

RESOURCE *Publications* · Eugene, Oregon

PALLIARE
Hard Edges and the Holy at the Edge of Life

Copyright © 2022 Marci Pounders. All rights reserved. Except for brief quotations in critical publications or reviews, no part of this book may be reproduced in any manner without prior written permission from the publisher. Write: Permissions, Wipf and Stock Publishers, 199 W. 8th Ave., Suite 3, Eugene, OR 97401.

Resource Publications
An Imprint of Wipf and Stock Publishers
199 W. 8th Ave., Suite 3
Eugene, OR 97401

www.wipfandstock.com

PAPERBACK ISBN: 978-1-6667-3504-8
HARDCOVER ISBN: 978-1-6667-9166-2
EBOOK ISBN: 978-1-6667-9167-9

04/19/22

*For all my teachers, mentors, patients,
and parishioners over the years.*

Who is there in all the world that listens to us? Here I am—this is me in my nakedness, with my wounds, my secret grief, my despair, my betrayal, my pain which I can't express, my terror, my abandonment. Oh, listen to me for a day, an hour, a moment, lest I expire in my terrible wilderness, my lonely silence. Oh God, is there no one to listen?

—DAME CICELY SAUNDERS,
founder of the modern hospice movement

Contents

List of Illustrations | ix
Introduction | xi

1. Is That Lipstick on Your Eyebrows? | 1
2. A Midwife to the Dying | 5
3. Piglet | 12
4. Starving for a Miracle | 17
5. The Tenth Leper | 22
6. From Hell to Eternity | 27
7. The Illusion of Control | 34
8. I'll Hold You Forever | 39
9. Blindsided | 45
10. A *Pietà* in the NICU | 50
11. Broken Heart Syndrome | 55
12. Jagged Little Secrets | 61
13. Sex and the Senior | 67
14. Communion, Disinfected | 72
15. All I Want is World Peace and a Pedicure | 77

Glossary | 87
Bibliography | 89

List of Illustrations

1. Ain't I a Dish?
2. Child of God
3. Holding You
4. Anorexia
5. Pretty Sick
6. Hope's Promise
7. Puppet on a String
8. Don't Worry I've Got You
9. Dark Blessings
10. Skull Cage
11. Raining Grief
12. Broken Heart
13. Jagged Little Secrets
14. Elder Love
15. Trapped

Introduction

MOST PEOPLE DO NOT consider what chaplain pastors in hospitals, hospices, or other care facilities do. You may assume that a chaplain pastor is simply someone who stops by a patient's room and sweetly offers a prayer. But you probably do not know that most hospital chaplains must have a master's degree or higher education from an accredited seminary, be ordained or endorsed by a religious body, and have completed at least four units of Clinical Pastoral Education to meet the requirements for professional chaplaincy. In addition, most hospitals require their chaplains to be professionally board certified through a national chaplaincy organization. Why? Because connecting with people's souls in times of crisis and death cannot be left to chance. One wrong word or action can change a patient's relationship with God forever. My work as a chaplain has changed mine.

We are ministers in the trenches of this battleground called life. We hold the heads and hands of patients who are bleeding to death. We sit in crowded emergency rooms with families anxiously awaiting news of a loved one's survival or death. We close the eyes of the dead. We hold waste baskets for hysterical family members vomiting uncontrollably. We perform weddings at the bedside of patients riddled with cancer and officiate at funerals of patients who have no other pastor. We assure them of God's love for them and we pray for those who, for whatever reason, cannot pray for themselves.

But it is in walking into such daily chaos that I have discovered incredible strength and beauty in people facing illness and death. Gifts of grief. Broken, courageous grace. I see God differently now. He walks with me down lonely hallways and sits with me in darkened rooms where the only sound is that of a respirator's forceful "whoosh." Jesus looks at me through the eyes of patients whose own eyes are dimmed with dementia or bright with fever. And the Holy Spirit, that marvelous Divine Feminine, holds me close and inspires me when I am close to falling apart.

This book is a collection of case studies I have worked as a chaplain in hospitals and hospice facilities, and as a priest in Episcopal parishes. I have taken appropriate measures to preserve privacy. But because I cannot make this stuff up, I pray that you are comforted, knowing you are not alone in your ponderings on life and death and the mysterious way God works in all of it.

The Rev. Dr. Marci Pounders
November 15, 2021

1

Is That Lipstick on Your Eyebrows?

DEMENTIA IS SUCH A terrible disease. It comes in many forms; Alzheimer's Disease, vascular dementia, stroke-related, drug-related, and way too many others. Whatever the cause, the result is always the same. The gradual loss of memory and physical ability leads to an inability to care for oneself, dependence on caregivers for all activities of daily living, a loss of contact with reality (this may include hallucinations, paranoia, and anxiety), reduction of appetite and desire to eat, and eventual death. Millions of dementia patients in the United States are in hospitals, care facilities and group homes because their families can no longer deal with their constant needs twenty-four hours a day.

There was one group home that housed four of our company's hospice patients. One was a lady with a beautiful smile. She no longer recognized anything. Her husband spent hours with her each day, waiting, hoping, praying to catch a glimpse of any cognitive light in her eyes. He would talk to her soothingly and spoon feed her a liquified lunch and she would respond with some unintelligible garble. But she smiled when he was around, and that was what he lived for. Another patient was an elderly man who was always watching classic television westerns with a bottle of Old Crow on his bedside table. He didn't talk much but he liked my company. We would watch the westerns together and I'd make him laugh by telling him that one day, we were going to have a major party with that bottle of whiskey. And one other patient was a very dignified old gentleman who was usually studying the daily newspaper upside down.

Then there was Mrs. D. Mrs. D was a tiny little old woman, shriveled up to almost nothing. But even with dementia, she was a force to be reckoned with. She kept her caregivers in her group home jumping. If she wanted something, she hollered. And whatever she wanted, she wanted it right then. You could hear her all over the facility. "Help! I need to get up!" "Where are my shoes?" Or more likely, "I want cookies!" She loved cookies. Cookies and sweet tea. That was all she would eat. Her patient aides would take care of her, and Mrs. D would be content until her next random urgent need. I felt for Mrs. D's poor roommate. But since I never, ever saw the roommate awake, I guess it didn't bother her too much.

Mrs. D called everyone on our hospice care team, "Hope." That was the name of our hospice service, and it was on our name badges, so we were all "Hope." "I like you, Hope," Mrs. D would say with a big toothless smile. "I like you too, Mrs. D," I'd reply. If the company nurse or social worker were visiting with me, she'd grab at their badges, stare at them and smile, "I like you, Hope." We never got tired of it. Mrs. D was a faithful Baptist and loved her Bible. She could no longer read it, but a well-worn copy was on her bedside table. She would parrot the same thing at every visit. "I'm Baptist and I love my Lord Jesus Christ." I'd read the Bible and we'd talk about Jesus, and she'd ask me about my family. "Hope, are you married?" I'd tell her about my husband and two children. Two minutes later she'd ask, "Hope, are you married?" She couldn't remember what she ate for breakfast most days, but she could remember, "I'm Baptist and I love my Lord Jesus Christ." And if that's all one can remember I suppose it's not a bad thing.

Mrs. D never failed to notice what I was wearing. "I like that dress." "I like your hair." "I like your eye shadow." One day, I happened to be wearing bright red lipstick (female chaplains need a pick me up occasionally). "I like that lipstick, Hope. I like that color red. Give me that." I had a tube in my purse, and I took it out. I was happy to show it to her and put a little on her lips. No *way* was I taking it back after it had touched her lips, so I screwed the cap back on and I let her hold it. She was so happy and excited. Again and again, she had to look at herself in her mirror. Then she had me wheel her out into the main corridor, waving that little gold tube so she could show herself off to everyone. The nurses made a big fuss over her. "Oh, Mrs. D! You are so gorgeous!" I checked with them that it was ok if I left the lipstick with her. "Of course," they said. She couldn't do much with it, as she didn't have the dexterity in her fingers to open the tube, and it certainly made her happy, so, sure. I left Mrs. D beaming in the dining room, gumming her cookies, and happily looking at the rosy lip marks on her frosty glass of sweet tea.

The next time I popped in to see Mrs. D, she was sitting in her room in her wheelchair with her back to the door. She was admiring herself in the mirror. Unfortunately, we had all misjudged both her physical abilities and her strong will. She had screwed open the cap of that lipstick with her gnarled, bony fingers and painted her eyebrows *bright red*. Not only that, but she had also painted the lips and eyebrows of her comatose roommate in the next bed. They both looked like nightmarish elderly clowns straight out of a Stephen King novel. Not stopping there, she had drawn horrifying red streaks on her dresser, tray table and mirror. If her aide came in right now, she would faint, thinking Mrs. D was bleeding to death. All I could think was, *Holy Sweet Mother of God*! I was going to get fired, blacklisted (red-listed in this case) from seeing any patients ever again, and all over a nine-dollar tube of Revlon!

"Mrs. D!" I blurted out. "Is that lipstick on your eyebrows?!" She gave me a naughty sideways glance. "Yeah! Ain't I a dish?" I sat down on the bed and laughed until I cried. Mrs. D laughed with me without understanding why. Then I found some wet wipes and cleaned up the room and the poor painted roommate before it all could be discovered, disposing of that unfortunate lipstick so no further such incidents could occur. As I gently wiped Mrs. D's face, she smiled. "I look so nice. Don't I look nice? I want some cookies. Are you married, Hope?" No one ever discovered what happened, Mrs. D's roommate never stirred, and I never, ever wore lipstick to that group home ever again.

2

A Midwife to the Dying

It takes a great deal of energy to die. Most people do not know this. They think death will look like what they have seen on television, a deathbed profession, a desperate last gasp, a sudden head-dropping-on-the-pillow, arm-dropping-off-the-bed type of end. I find this silly, because even in hospital emergency rooms, I have not found death to be like this. Even in traumatic circumstances, the end when it does come, is rarely so dramatic. One lives until one does not. The heart gradually stops, the ragged breath goes. That is the way of all the earth. I was privileged to travel this last journey with a hospice patient I'll call "Mami." Mami was an elderly Latina woman who had breast and colon cancer. She also suffered from chronic diabetes and kidney failure. This time, she had not been able to bounce back, and she was failing. She was admitted to our in-patient hospice unit to be kept comfortable until the end.

When I first visited Mami, she was semi-lucid, but very agitated. This is common in patients with less than a week to live. Her neurological transmitters were beginning to shut down. She kept trying to get out of bed until the pain medication sedated her. When she did open her eyes, there was a wide, blank, almost bewildered stare into nothingness. When she closed her eyes again, she smiled and appeared to be carrying a conversation with someone.

Palliare

Her daughter J whispered, "She's talking with my dad. He died two years ago. She says that he is putting on his tuxedo to meet her. He's going to take her to a party, but he's being slow about it, and she's aggravated he's late." Her daughter managed a tired smile. "He was always late, wasn't he, Mami?" Mami was seeing things we could not see. "How wonderful," I said. "She's going to be with him soon and he's there anticipating her arrival." "Yes," replied J. "That makes me happy, to know they'll soon be together."

I have always been fascinated by deathbed hallucinations. Are they real? To the dying person, they are very real. My own mother was convinced there were toucans roosting in the ceiling of her intensive care room. One of my patients years ago was terrified of the wolves she believed were lurking outside her hospital room door. (My pastoral care duty on that visit was to shoo the wolves away and stand guard). Another patient saw ghouls that he described as looking like Gollum, from the *Lord of the Rings* movies. Another saw angels. One saw a beautiful woman floating at the foot of her bed. And yet another was convinced that the lovely painting of red poppies in his hospital room was a picture of Satan smoking pot. I could not convince him otherwise.

The brain does strange things when one is dying. Of course, medications such as morphine, propofol, methadone and fentanyl can cause hallucinations. And urinary tract infections and a lack of oxygen and blood to the brain are also to blame. But I have been with too many dying people seeing angels, heaven, deceased loved ones and even Jesus to think that God in his infinite mercy does not reach out in some mysterious way to comfort his children on their way home to him. I wished so much that I could glimpse the mystery that my dying patient was seeing!

J was so very tired. She was her mother's only child, and there was no one else to relieve her long days at the hospital. She insisted on staying around the clock, because Mami would become anxious if J was not within her line of sight. One day, J asked me, "I don't know what to expect. I've never done this before. My dad died of a heart attack, and we didn't have to camp out at the hospital all

A Midwife to the Dying

day and night like this," she said. "What will it, you know, *death*, look like?"

I thought of a classic episode of the old television show, *The Twilight Zone*, where the Angel of Death (a very young and ridiculously handsome Robert Redford) comes gently to a frightened elderly woman. I didn't tell J that I sincerely hope on the day I pass from this earth that my death angel will look like a young, tanned, ridiculously handsome George Clooney. "J, every person's death is unique to them." I talked gently about the usual signs and symptoms associated with one's last days. There would be a gradual decline from agitation to somnolence, more hallucinations, loss of appetite, slowed, labored breathing, a shutting down of urine output, and finally the cessation of heartbeat and breath. "Yes, but does it hurt? Will she be in pain? Will she get hungry or thirsty? Should I feed her? What should I do?"

The most distressing thing to most folks is when their loved ones stop eating and drinking. We associate food with life, with love, with holidays and the celebration of happy times. We think we are not doing enough to keep our dear one alive, or that they will "starve to death" without food. But when a person is dying, his or her body uses up every bit of energy it has just trying to keep breathing and to keep the heart pumping. Digestion takes away from this, and it diverts energy away from the brain. Palliative physicians advocate for "comfort feeding" such as popsicles, pudding, ice cream, milkshakes, or whatever the patient truly might want while they are still able to enjoy it. I once got take-out Kentucky Fried Chicken for a patient with the physician's permission. She gummed away at it happily with the one tooth left in her mouth. But if a person is actively dying, food can cause more discomfort when it is forced. "You just need to be here," I reassured J. "She's being kept comfortable with pain medication. Death shouldn't hurt at all. Just like a deep sleep and a transition to the eternal. If she wants something, of course by all means give it to her. But don't force her. Her body knows exactly what it needs right now." J was somewhat less anxious about what to expect.

Palliare

The next day, Mami was remarkably awake and aware of her surroundings. She knew she was in the hospital. She didn't know who I was at first, but after about ten minutes, she understood that I was the chaplain, and I was okay to be there. I think what made me more "okay" was the big sparkly necklace I was wearing. Mami loved jewelry. She kept looking at me saying, "That's so pretty!" She would look at me, then back at her daughter. She would smile at J. Then she'd look back at me. "Oh, that is so pretty!" like she'd never seen me or my necklace before. I took the necklace off and let her hold it. When she didn't want to give it back, J was horrified. "Oh, Mami! No! That's the chaplain's jewelry!" Mami frowned and clutched it tighter. "No, it's not! It's *mine*!" When J started to take the necklace back, I quietly gestured no. Arguing with patients who are confused or have dementia never works. It only makes them more upset. It was ok, I whispered to J. I could get it later. Then I told Mami how much we had in common, to like pretty things. She nodded and smiled contentedly.

Dying patients often rally and have one last big burst of energy before slipping into their final coma. The following day, Mami was very talkative. She held court with family and friends in the morning, oriented times ten. Then in the afternoon, she crumped (medical slang for failing fast). J put in an urgent call for me. Mami snorted that I was *not* the chaplain; I was someone else. Soon I had morphed into a friend from church and then a cousin who had been dead for years. J gently corrected her again and again. Finally, Mami looked at me and said, "Oh yes, she's the pastor, isn't she?" And we all smiled. Suddenly out of nowhere, Mami farted. And I don't mean a cute little fart. I mean an *Enormous Ghastly From The Depths of Hell Fart*. The aroma was powerful enough to peel the paint off the walls. J and I giggled, even as our eyes were watering. Mami's eyes grew wide, and she looked just like a naughty child caught in mischief. Shocked, Mami whispered, "Oh! I did it! It was me!" "You bad girl!" we joked and scolded. And our sweet patient laughed too, for what else can one do? You can laugh or you can cry. Both have their place, but in this case, it was more comforting to laugh. Then she needed the bedpan (we certainly just had ample warning!) and we called the nurse.

Mami did not want us to leave her sight, even while she was using the bedpan. Honestly, neither J nor I cared. It was simply a part of life, this uncontrollable urge, this reversion to babyhood, this helplessness. We didn't want her to be any more agitated or embarrassed than she already was, so we let the nurse do her job, and we moved to another corner of the room to talk about nothing. "Mi hija!" "I'm here Mami." "Where? I can't see you!" "Right here, Mami. See, Marci's here too." Mami took my hand and sobbed. "I'm so sorry. I'm so sorry. I'm so sorry." "What for, Mami?" I knew what for. She was lucid enough to realize she had shit her bed, and someone had to clean her up. She was losing control. She was mortified. She didn't want to be here. "I love you so much," said Mami asking forgiveness for her helplessness. "I love you, too," I said, as I patted her hand.

The next day, Mami thought the trees waving outside the window were people. She saw her deceased husband, waiting for her. She spoke exclusively in Spanish, the language of her birth. She could not understand that I, not knowing much Spanish, couldn't answer her. "Mami, this is Marci. She is the chaplain. She doesn't speak Spanish." Mami shook her head and continued her conversation. It sounded most interesting. She was very certain about what and to whom she was talking. I could make out she was praying at some point. Then her eyes closed, and she gave herself over to her deep exhaustion. A great struggle was going on inside of her. She knew deep down she was dying, and something in her longed to go. But she was worried about J. Who would take care of her? She was J's mother and mothers worry about their babies, even if they are grown. "I love you so much," she repeated over and over. "I'm so sorry." J and I sat with her for hours in silence. I think that's why Mami asked for me by name. When she was disoriented, I didn't push her back to reality. I didn't talk too much. I didn't correct her. I didn't startle her. And I was not loud. Dying people do not like loud noises or loud voices. It is just too much for their short-circuiting senses. Dying people need holy silence and sacred

Palliare

presence while they labor because death is so much like birth. Being with Mami was like witnessing a birth where the mother is not yet completely dilated. Something big was about to happen, and she was struggling to get through it, but it was not time yet to push. Every movement that Mami made, every twitch, every start, every squirm, looked like a woman in labor. She was birthing into a new existence, surrendering to uncertainty and an utter lack of control. It was not sudden or dramatic nor was it easy. It took all her energy. It left her spent.

The last time I saw Mami, she was no longer responsive. Her breathing was slowing down, heavy with mucus, what old timers call the "death rattle," and what modern physicians refer to as Cheyne-Stokes respiration. J was by her side, holding her hand. "She's in her final hours now. Her kidneys are shutting down." J motioned to the empty bedside catheter. "Thank you for being here with us." Mami was at peace. She had given birth and was now waiting for the afterbirth and the cord of life finally to be severed. I have no doubt that she knows J will be all right, for I have seen so many dying souls come to this place of peace. I have no doubt that Mami will be carried up to God on angel's wings. And I know her husband is fully dressed in his best formal attire, ready and waiting for her with open arms, to take her to the biggest party of her life where they will dance, feast, and love again in the courtyard of God's kingdom.

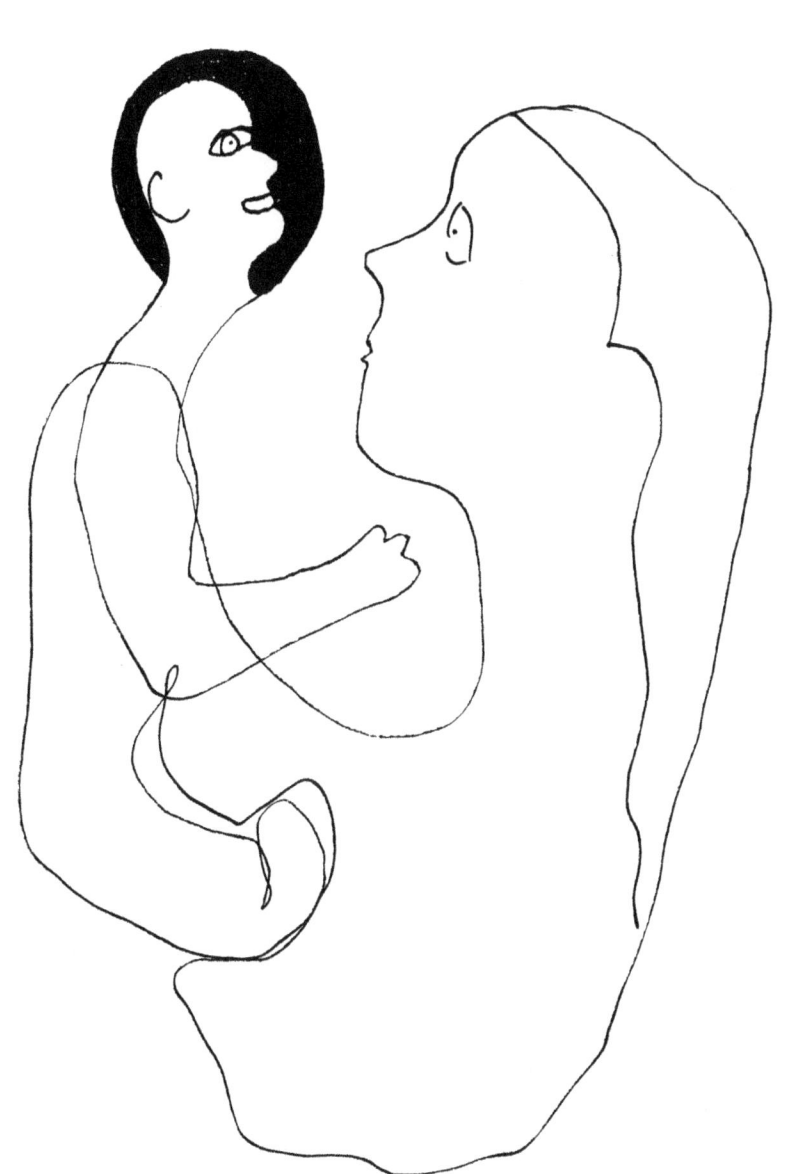

── 3 ──

Piglet

It was midnight on my overnight chaplain shift at the county hospital. I had been in Labor and Delivery, waiting for a fetal demise. That is the cold sterile hospital term for a stillbirth. The baby had not yet been delivered, and the parents were not yet ready to see a chaplain. Things were unusually quiet. I received a fax referral for a premature infant in the Neonatal Intensive Care Unit, so I walked over to visit the preemie and see the other little babies in the unit. After scrubbing, putting on a protective plastic gown and gloving up, I swiped my badge to enter the unit. "Hi, I'm the chaplain on duty tonight. May I come in to visit our little ones?" The nurse waved me in. "Sure, Chaplain. Come on in." The Neo-Natal Intensive Care Unit was very quiet. The lights were dimmed, and the only sounds were of the ventilators and other life-sustaining machinery. Whoosh, beep. Whoosh, beep. Whoosh, beep. The nurses all moved slowly and gently, and if they spoke at all, it was very softly. Such a contrast to the noise of the other hospital units. "I just received a fax referral for a Baby G. Is he here in this unit?" The nurse looked puzzled. "Hmmm. I don't recall that one. Oh yes, he has just come in. He's right here." She pointed to the bassinet next to the door. "OK, thanks. I need to make a note that I've seen him." Such a tiny baby, all swaddled up like a miniature cocoon. His

Piglet

little blue knit cap overwhelmed the wrinkled crimson head, blue veins coursing through his translucent skin. Funny how preemies look like wizened little old men, I thought. I looked at all the little beings in the incubators. Unfortunately, it was a full house tonight.

I asked the nurse if I could visit a bit. "Of course," she replied. She was busy checking on one baby in the very back of the room. She spoke to the baby lovingly. "Yes, I know! You tell me about it!" She laughed and smiled, leaning over the bassinet so the baby could see her face. I came over for a closer look. And my heart completely melted.

In the crib was a tiny infant, propped up on a small pillow. The baby had a breathing tube, which was as big around as his own little throat. His facial deformities were startling, a cleft palate and no lower jaw. But his huge dark eyes were bright and his manner spunky. He tried to smile, which looked funny with no lower jaw. I smiled back and began to talk to him. He responded by wiggling and patting his miniscule hand against a stuffed toy. Again, he tried to smile, which came across as a grimace. Then he snorted. That was part of the way he breathed on the ventilator, but it was so comical that both the nurse and I cracked up. He sounded just like a tiny pig.

I let him hold my finger, which was huge in comparison to his hand. He grabbed it weakly and held on for a moment. Then he dropped it and snorted again. "He's being so feisty tonight!" The nurse laughed. I laughed too. He snorted again. I snorted back. He snorted in response, wiggling and grimacing. For a few amazing moments, we communicated in this odd manner, with snorting, finger holding, smiles, coos, and grimaces. The baby locked eyes with me as if I was very interesting. He knew I was a new face. The nurse was delighted and giggled along with us. "This little guy is special. He's one of my favorites," she said. "I can see why. He's adorable," I replied "How old is he?" "Almost four months. But he only weighs seven pounds. We might be able to fix his cleft palate, but with no lower mandibles, it would be a challenge. Plus, he has a bad heart. Everything is wrong with his heart. I don't even know if a transplant would work. He's so weak." The nurse drifted off in thought. "And he's got so many other cards stacked against him. Bad heart,

Palliare

facial deformities. His mother's only fifteen. She lives out in West Texas and can't afford to get here to Dallas." Piglet (as I now called him) wiggled mightily, waving his little fists and snorting, as if to remind us, "Hey! I'm *here*!" His nurse returned his attention. "I know, Buddy. I see you! You're precious, yes you are!" She sighed. "He's not expected to live six months." If my heart had melted before, it now puddled at my feet, offering a sad reflection of reality. "Oh." I struggled to speak. "Poor little guy." "Yep," the nurse said softly, stroking the baby's head. "I hate it. He's just so sweet."

We stood around the crib in silence for a long time. Finally, I spoke. "How hard is this for you? I mean, how hard is it for you to care for babies you know will die?" The nurse reflected a moment. "It's hard. I think it's a bit easier for us nurses who have been here awhile. I've been here thirteen years. I'm older. I've seen a lot. But it's harder for the younger ones. They want to take each one home with them, or they get too emotionally attached." She kept stroking Piglet's head. He wiggled and grimaced, obviously loving the attention. She paused. "It just seems wrong, doesn't it? I mean, here you have a baby that was loved and wanted. Mom did everything right, even though she was so young. And then you have drug addict moms who abuse and neglect the kids they do have, and they just keep having more and they're born ok. Sort of. Sometimes. Or they get thrown away in dumpsters or flushed down the toilet." The nurse sighed. "Anyway, it just seems wrong. This little guy did not do anything to be born like this. He didn't ask for such a bad deal."

No, he did not. And the age-old question of "Why?" remained unanswered for me. Why do bad things happen to good people? Why are innocent babies born with defects? I had struggled with this concept for twenty years, ever since my own little daughter was born with a brain injury. *She* didn't deserve it. *I* didn't deserve it. I had cried a river of tears then, and my faith in God was shaken to the core. It was so shaken that I left the church I had been attending since birth. It was a prosperity gospel church that placed a great deal of emphasis on positive thinking and denial of anything negative. People told me to deny the power of the seizures and to think positively so they would go away. Of course, the seizures did *not* go away. I strongly believe in the power of prayer, but it was impossible to deny away my toddler unresponsive in *status epilepticus* so badly that I was forced to call an ambulance. I soon realized I had to be an advocate for my child, as well as my own spiritual journey. I needed a God that could wipe my tears and cry along with me. So, I quit church. *"Screw this. God, where are you? Are you even listening?"* It was a long time before I could pray or attend services at any church again.

When I found the Episcopal Church, I started to breathe again. I took such great comfort in the Eucharistic prayers, the liturgy, and the sacraments. It was mysterious. It was holy. It was healing. I did not know exactly why at the time, but I felt I did not need to know why. It fed my soul. I wanted to learn more. So, I enrolled in seminary, was trained in Christian theology, homiletics, systematics, liturgics, spiritual direction, pastoral care, and biblical Greek. Eventually I became an Episcopal priest. But becoming ordained in and of itself does not give you all the answers to life's mysterious conundrums. I wish it did.

"Yes, it does seem wrong," I agreed sadly. The nurse shrugged. But she smiled as Piglet snorted and waved his fists aimlessly, calling attention to himself yet again. We stood by his bassinet, the nurse stroking his head, while I held his tiny hand with my finger. He looked intently at both of us. It was as if that baby knew we needed some sort of hope, some sign of reassurance, some answer to the "Why?" And it was in that moment that I knew that I did not need an answer. God's presence shone brightly through that baby's big, dark eyes. Love, trust, wisdom, struggle, suffering, victory, all of it! The mystery of Jesus's life, death and resurrection were right here in this crib, and I marveled at God's self-giving. Bad things happen thanks to physics, evolution, and poor choices. But God is present even in the ugliness of life. God is with us in our weakness and deformities. The greatest grace is that in our woundedness, we may draw closer to the Crucified One who loves without exception. There would be a cross for this baby, and for those who loved him, but not this night. This night was one where I, in the guise of a humble shepherd, would worship at a nativity in the NICU.

— 4 —

Starving for a Miracle

SHE WOULD HAVE BEEN a strikingly beautiful woman if she had any muscle tone left in her face, any joy in her lifeless eyes. Fifty-one years old, five feet ten inches, seventy-one pounds. She was my age and yet she looked eighty. A thirty-eight-year battle with anorexia had left her exhausted, spent, and psychologically scarred. I looked at her in the hospital bed. She was receiving intravenous fluids, so she had energy enough to talk. But she was as colorless and skeletal as a fuzzy black-and-white Eisenstadt photo from Auschwitz. Every ligament in her fragile throat, every bone in her wasted form was visible. A loss of just one or two more pounds would kill her. Even while she begged me for help, I sensed that she did not really seem to care. *My God, I thought. What is eating her?*

As I came to know her, I discovered that Ms. A was consumed by feelings of unworthiness. She never felt pretty enough, thin enough, smart enough, good enough. Gradually, these feelings of worthlessness translated into a desperate bid for control. She told me that it started early in her life. She felt unloved and unappreciated. She told me of a childhood filled with taunts and teasing. At one time she was "fat." She enjoyed food and took pleasure in meals. Now, she cannot remember the last time she touched meat, or the last time she ate a "normal" meal. She is no longer hungry. Once and for all, she is in control. Once and for all, she is out of control.

First it was the refusal of a meal. Then she added compulsive exercise. Food was eventually rejected entirely as the glory of finally being "thin" was savored. Gradually, she denied herself all forms of pleasure. Love, sexual intimacy, employment, and ordinary living became impossible as the hedonism of control took over. Her manipulation of family and friends destroyed any remaining relationships. Every waking moment hinged on her next meal and what **not** to eat. Now, the effects of long-term chronic starvation were causing her body to feed off its own muscles and tissues. The palliative medicine physician had given Ms. A one strong, no-nonsense lecture on what would happen if she continued to refuse food. Two more pounds. Her life hung in the balance. Two more pounds, and her organs would shut down. Two more pounds and she would die.

Anorexia is a complicated and selfish disease. In most cases, it is a distraction from mental and emotional pain. Ms. A was a classic case. She had lived her life frightened and inhibited. Her bid for control turned into iron-clad aggressiveness. She was angry at others for failing to help her but loathe to blame herself for what she had become. Ms. A told everyone who would listen that she wanted help. She cried as she described the failure of her marriage, friends who had given up on her and finances on edge due to constant illnesses and hospitalizations. "I got married in my twenties. I thought maybe then I could be happy. But I couldn't have children. My husband left me then, said he could not deal with me anymore. Everyone has abandoned me! I guess I deserve it."

Jesus, she was so pitiful. "Everyone?" I queried. "Do you believe God has abandoned you too?" "Please help me!" she begged. "I've prayed and prayed for God to help me. But he doesn't. I don't know why." She did not seem to grasp the idea that maybe God was waiting for her to help herself. She reminded me of the story of the crippled man in the Gospel of John who had waited for thirty-eight years to get into the healing pool at Siloam (John 5:1–9). The pool was believed to have healing properties because it bubbled up on a regular basis. It was thought that if you got into the pool when it foamed up, you would be healed of your infirmity. The crippled man had sat by that healing spring for most of his life, yet he had done nothing to help himself and even with Jesus standing right in front of him, he still managed to blame everyone else for his own inaction. More importantly, he never answered Jesus's question, "Do you want to be made well?" Ms. A cried out for help repeatedly. But I never once heard her say she *wanted to be made well*. She was far too stuck in her utter dependence on everyone, far too warped emotionally to blame herself, and she hated the world for "not helping her." Yet Christ had come to her over and over in the guise of treatment specialists, doctors, and patient caregivers to offer help. She did not recognize him. She denied him.

"Please help me!" She gripped my hand surprisingly tightly for one so ill. "You understand. You can help me, can't you?" I looked at her untouched lunch tray. I had worked a long shift and I was hungry. Her chicken salad sandwich looked awfully good to me. How hard could it be to eat it? *"Oh, for God's sake, just eat the damn sandwich!"* I thought. But she couldn't. I offered to feed her small pieces of it, but she refused. "I don't want that." Then I thought of something that maybe she would want. I pulled a pyx out of my pocket, a little silver circular box that holds blessed communion wafers. "Do you know what this is?" I asked her. She shook her head no. I took out a wafer. "This is holy food. The Body of Christ. Would you be willing to try this?" She nodded yes. I watched as she took the wafer very, very carefully in her hands. She was so dehydrated, I wondered if she could even get it down. Then an amazing thing happened. It took her about five minutes, but she ate that wafer. She broke off tiny, tiny pieces of it. I could not help but contrast it to how most worshipers receive it. Kneel. Gulp. Cross ourselves. Done. But not this time. I watched as a miracle unfolded before me. Very, very slowly she took miniscule bites. Her eyes closed, and her face took on a new radiance. Tiny bite, chew, swallow. Tiny bite, chew, swallow. She was *savoring* this bread of heaven, smiling, tears running down her thin cheeks. For one moment she had surrendered control. She was truly entering into the holiest of Communions. It did not matter that her tray table was filled with uneaten soup and applesauce. It had become a holy altar where the Most High had touched his child, filled her with manna, and satiated her. I fervently prayed that this would lead to a spiritual breakthrough.

I visited with Ms. A several more times before she was discharged. Most of the time, I had to chase her down in the hallway. Even tethered to her IV and barely able to stand, she walked in endless circles around the unit hanging on to her walker, still compulsively exercising. We always had the same talk. She always wanted help, and I always gave her a communion wafer. For all I know, it was the last solid food she accepted. She died a few weeks later.

Thirty-eight years is a long time to suffer. I wonder what Ms. A thought when she finally found herself in heaven, with the ultimate feast before her. Did she take her place proudly at the Lord's Table? When God himself welcomed her into his fellowship of plenty and all the good things he had prepared for her, did she accept the plate and cup from the hands of the Master? Or did she refuse, believing herself worthy of only a few crumbs that fell overflowing from the plates of others? The choice was hers.

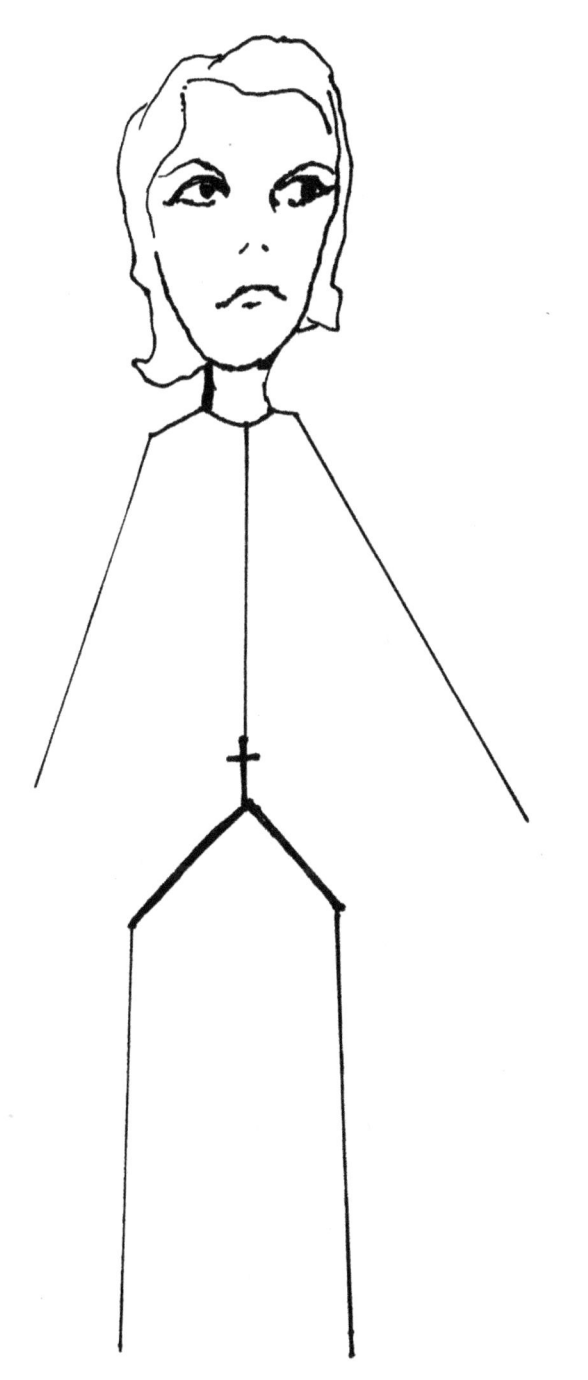

— 5 —

The Tenth Leper

A COUPLE OF YEARS ago, I encountered the tenth leper.

His name was Mr. B and he was a hospice patient I met on rounds at his facility. Mr. B was an elderly Black man. When he found out I was a pastor, he eagerly opened up to me about his life. It was a hard life of drinking, drugs, family struggles, violence and prison time. He didn't sugar coat it, either. He was clearly used to life on the streets or in a jail cell. The tell-tale prison tattoos on his arms (always that same weird mimeograph blue) testified to his doing time.

Mr. B was dying of terminal liver cancer. Yet his reaction to this news was not what I expected. No denial. No anger. No blaming himself or others. Instead, he was calm, even cheerful. "When the Lord says, *go*, I'll go. Ain't no use to struggle. He'll take me when He's ready." I saw a well-worn Bible at his side, and I asked him about his faith. Obviously, something had happened in his life to turn him from a criminal into this gentle man beside me, radiating peace. So, he told me his story.

Mr. B's life bore the scars of poverty and ignorance. As a younger man, he didn't have any real faith or a relationship with God. He hung around with the wrong crowd. He drank, did drugs. Became a petty thief. Got caught stealing from the boss. "I know'd

The Tenth Leper

it was wrong. I know'd it. Did it anyway. Just needed the money." He shrugged. He was sent to prison for his crime. Just another Black man in the pen. Just another forgotten statistic.

"But it was goin' to jail that saved me," continued Mr. B. He had enough education to read, and the prison chaplain gave him a Bible. Mr. B didn't have much else to do, so he read it. From cover to cover. Something got hold of him, he said. He wasn't sure what, but the story of the apostle Paul in chains shook him to the core. He took the words of 2 Timothy to heart. *"But the word of God is not chained. Therefore I endure everything for the sake of the elect, so that they may also obtain the salvation that is in Christ Jesus, with eternal glory."* One night, he had a vision. "I saw a light, like a waterfall, right there on the prison wall. I knew if I could just get to that light, I'd be a different man. I stood in that light, that waterfall and let it wash me clean. I was baptized and saved, right then in that moment." His smile was glorious.

Now I've heard a lot of stories in my time, with patients who are medicated, or who have a past history of addiction, or who are manipulative and excellent liars. Oh, I've heard some doozies. But as I listened, I could hear in my mind the strains of an old Motown blues song, "One of these days, one of these days, I shall be released." My curiosity got the better of me. I wanted to hear what happened after this so-called "baptism." "Well, my cell mate thought I'd gone stark raving mad. He didn't know what had happened to me. *He didn't know.* He didn't have *faith.* He couldn't *see.*" To prove his point, Mr. B began evangelizing. To anyone who would listen. He preached in the prison yard during exercise time. He preached to his cellmate. He read the Bible aloud at meals. And he annoyed the heck out of everyone. They slapped him in solitary, thinking he was crazy. He continued to read the Bible, from cover to cover. Seven times. Each time they'd let him out, he'd start preaching again. And he'd be put back in solitary.

Eventually, Mr. B served his time. He got out, reunited with his wife and family, and became an elder in a small Baptist church. Then cancer caught up with him. Although unlikely, he was hoping to get back to church one day if his health permitted. He was writing a sermon the morning I visited, and he proudly shared his sermon with me. It was difficult to read, due to misspellings, and poor handwriting, but the words were powerful, written in the cadence of the call-and-response so often found in the Black church. His text was the story of the poor man in hell begging Abraham to warn his brothers to mend their ways.

As I read his sermon aloud, (I'm a good dramatic reader, by the way), I got into the rhythm. "Am I right?" "Did ya hear that?" "If ya heard the *Word*, give me an amen!" Mr. B was delighted that I "got it," and he responded right along with me; "Oh yes, Lord! Amen! Thank you, Jesus!" I'm telling you, we were having church right there in that hospice room. Even the nurses had gathered out in the hallway to listen. And then the clincher. "*Tell hell I ain't comin'*!"

"*Tell hell I ain't comin'*!" "Amen!" echoed the nurses in the hall.

The words jumped out at me. A proclamation of faith and certainty from a man who was facing a very grim prognosis. "What do you mean by that, Mr. B?" I asked. He raised his grizzled eyebrows and looked at me as if to say, "What kind of a pastor *are* you?" "I mean Jesus Christ of course," he snorted. "It was Jesus that saved me in prison. Jesus got me out of prison. He healed my heart. And now that my body's goin', He's gonna give me eternal life. I'm not afraid." There it was again, that old blues song in my mind, "One of these days, one of these days, I shall be released." I paused as the power of those words sunk in.

"Prison, solitary. Now cancer. You've suffered hell on earth, Mr. B." He nodded. "Oh yes. I've been in hell. But now I got heaven to look forward to. That's why I say, 'Tell hell I ain't comin.'" He shook his head. "*I ain't comin*'! I thank God every day for the good things I've had."

I thought of the story of the ten lepers in Luke 17, where Jesus encounters a group of lepers and heals them. Nine rejoiced and went their way. But only one turned back to Jesus and remembered to thank him. Mr. B reminded me of this leper. Because, let's face it, criminals and street people are the lepers of society. They are outcasts, rejected, not welcome in "polite company." You could even say he was, metaphorically, a Samaritan, foreign to the ways of God, worshipping the wrong kinds of gods: alcohol, drugs, money. Yet here was a man who turned back to the Holy Presence that always welcomes us. Like the prodigal son, the Father welcomed him with open arms.

He paused, and then reflected, "I'm trustin' him to look after my family when I'm gone. I don't want no fussin', and no fightin'. My family, they fights a bit. And I'm gonna tell my family they gotta trust in him. They gotta thank him, or they won't get where I'm goin." He pointed a thin finger skyward. Just then the telephone rang, and he had to take the call, so I took my leave. I did not see Mr. B again.

Some might say that there are no atheists in the trenches. Some might say that this man was simply playing off my sympathy, or in denial, or had a psychological problem. But I don't think so. Mr. B radiated the peace and assurance of something better coming, of hope, not anger; not vindictiveness or even a fear of divine reprisal for his past misdeeds. No, this man was a powerful testimony to the inner joy that God brings when the heart is healed by faith.

Mr. B's renewed faith and his transformation in prison are testimonies to the Lord's steadfast love and loyalty. How many of us can claim such a glorious baptism of light? Oh, how I wish I had been able to see Mr. B, arms outstretched, tears running down his cheeks, accepting the Master's forgiving grace! For how many of us can, with complete assurance, know that "One of these days, one of these days, I shall be released?"

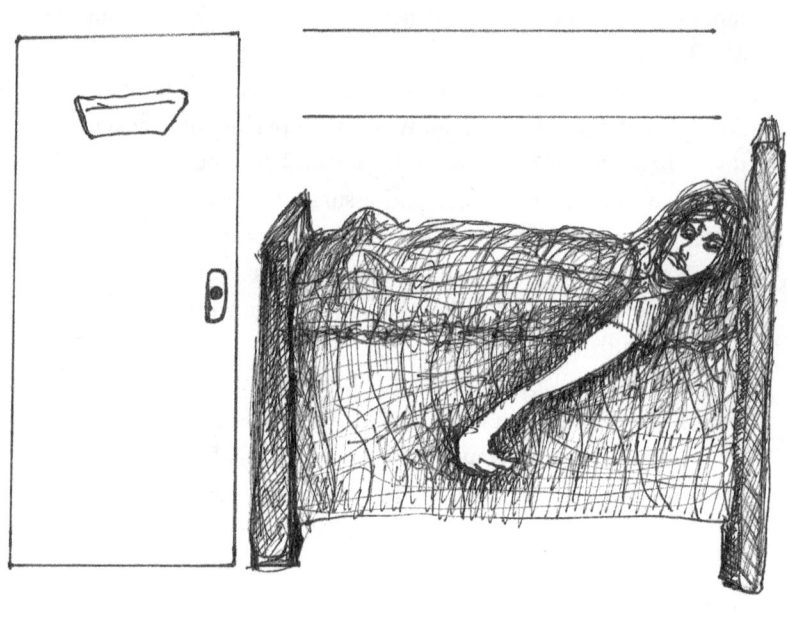

— 6 —

From Hell to Eternity

I ONCE WORKED FOR a palliative care physician who was fond of saying that death is not so much a physical problem to be solved as it is a spiritual problem to be resolved. The spiritual aspect of dying can confound us, even when, as Christians, we have been taught that there is a glorious heaven waiting for us. When we start to obsess over various sins that we may have committed, real or imagined, guilt leads us to believe we deserve the Almighty's wrath. Even worse, when death is knocking at the door, we may suddenly and totally become frightened by the horrible thought that there may not be a heaven like we have always been taught or that we've imagined. What if there is not *anything*? What if all we are facing is not divine light and comfort, but darkness and nothingness? Like Tolstoy's character, Ivan Ilyich, we may deny the entire idea of death in silent protest, "I shall be no more, what does it mean? For where, indeed shall I be when I shall be no more? Can it be death? No, I will not die."[1] Or worse, we may believe we are condemned to a sulfurous burning hell. I never fail to be saddened that many good people believe that our loving God will abandon us in our last moments and not be there for us in eternity.

---

1. Tolstoy, *Death of Ivan Ilyich*, 42.

Palliare

One particularly busy day at the hospital, the palliative care doctor came to me. "I don't know quite how to approach this patient," he said. "She is absolutely terrified. Her faith background is Christian, but she won't talk to me about it. In fact, she won't talk much to anyone. She seems so lost and afraid." The doctor explained that this patient had come from out of state to await a liver transplant, but upon reaching the hospital, she was too weak to be a viable candidate. "Is it disappointment?" I ventured. "No, it's more than that. I am not sure, but she seems more terrified of what will happen to her *after* she dies, rather than the actual process of death itself. I think that's more up your alley than mine, Chaplain." When I arrived at the room, the charge nurse concurred. "They have just told her there's not much more they can do. I feel so bad for her." The nurse's face fell. She was as concerned as the doctor. "She and her husband are both in there crying. I've told her we can take care of her pain, but she just won't open herself up to us. Maybe you can help her?" I agreed to try. I entered the room with the nurse. The room was dark, the blinds drawn as if the sunlight itself was fearful of piercing the gloom. In the corner, a plump old gentleman sat hunched in a chair, quietly wiping his eyes. The patient was in bed, stone-faced, staring at the ceiling. Her yellowed skin only added to the grey-beige palette of depression.

The nurse introduced me briefly and beat a quick retreat. The patient's husband sobbed softly, "We've had some bad news." I listened as the patient's husband did most of the talking. The patient laid there, tears streaming down her cheeks. I went over to the bedside, wiped the woman's tears, and took her hand. "I'm not ready, I'm not ready," she whispered. Her voice trailed off. For a moment, only the sound of soft sobs filled the hospital room. Then she turned her head and looked desperately at me. "I'm not ready to die! I'm so afraid!" When one suddenly is faced with dying, the unknown smacks you in the face and mocks your faith in the eternal. "I'm not ready for this! The nurse told me hospice is my only option. Hospice! That means I'm dying, and . . . then I'll go to hell!" Tears continued to well up and spill over her sunken eyelids. "It's a burning place, with fire and sulfur and terrible things! I'm not good enough to get into heaven. And I'll never see my husband again! He's such a good man, I *know* he will get into heaven! But not me! And I just can't stand the thought I won't be with him ever again!" As I held the woman's hand, I was not quite sure what to say to her. She turned away. She was leaving go out of state on hospice care the next day. I might not see her again. I lifted up a silent prayer and plunged in between the allegorical rock of her hospital bed and the hard place we were about to go together. "Tell me why you believe you will go to hell," I ventured. She calmed down enough to talk. "Well," she sighed, "I just know I'm not good enough." Tears continued to flow down her jaundiced cheeks. "I came here to get a new liver, and now I'm too weak for a transplant and there's no hope." Her eyes were dull, blurred with devastation. Her husband, sitting in a chair beside the bed, began to cry, too. "I had a stroke, about three years go," he choked. He was silent for a moment. He struggled to speak. "She's taken care of me ever since, and now she's going to leave me!" He could not go on and left the room, choking on his sobs.

I thought of another patient I had visited in her home. She had hung on to the delicate curtain of her life with every ounce of her waning strength, clutching at it, tearing at it while it steadily ripped away. Her daughters told me she was afraid because she doubted. She wondered if everything she had been told in church was a lie, that there would be nothing, that her deceased husband would not be there for her. So, she would not let go. Only with her daughters gently holding her hand and whispering in her ear that they would place her hand directly into that of her late husband's and not let go until she crossed over, did she finally pass away.

So, what spiritual reassurance could I give this poor woman? That I believe Thomas really was the most beloved disciple precisely *because* he doubted? That the dark is not always a bad dark, but a holy silence, a quiet divine embrace, a time of transition? Should I share words from the Episcopal burial rites, "I am the Resurrection, and I am Life, says the Lord. Whoever has faith in me shall have life, even though he dies?" Or my favorite Bible verses commonly read at funerals, such as Psalm 139 or John 14:1–6?

Palliare

How could I convince her that God knew her intimately, knit her together in her mother's womb, and offered her a spiritual haven with many rooms and surely there would be one for her? That there was a heaven precisely because Jesus loved her enough to go down into hell himself to claim her? Intercessory prayer can be a powerful tool in conveying confidence and reassurance. When one is not strong enough to pray for oneself, the mediation of the Holy Spirit can make all the difference, both in spoken word and silent presence. So, I called upon her to help this woman believe in her own sacred worthiness.

"Why do you think you aren't good enough for God?" I asked gently. She turned back to me wearily. "I'm not worthy." she sighed. "What have you done in your life that could possibly make God not love you?" I wondered. Was it abuse, a secret abortion, an unkind word, a horrible mistake? It is tragic how we magnify the wrongs we have done until they become the biggest, most monstrous Giant Godzilla Sin ever to lay waste to whatever Good Tokyo Karma we have built up. And it is even more tragic how those in authority will prey upon the vulnerable, holding them captive to an ideal of holiness that no real person can ever attain. Thirty years of fear. That is no way to live. Or die. I took her shriveled hand firmly in mind. "What makes you think that God, who created you as his beautiful child, wouldn't love you enough to welcome you home into his kingdom?" Her eyes grew wide. "Do you think so? Oh, that's what I want! I want it so much! But what about hell? Don't you believe in a burning hell?" "No," I said slowly. "I believe the pain of separation from God is worse than any burning could be." I paused. "It's been this way for you, hasn't it?" She bent her head, clutched her blanket, and sighed, nodding. I leaned in a bit closer and touched her thin cheek. "Jesus doesn't wish this for you. He is with you, right now, right here, with his arms around you." Together, we talked about how she might reframe her fears into an ideal of her own human worth. We looked at each other imploringly—she desperately wanting to believe me; me desperately wanting her to accept Jesus's reconciling grace. For a miraculous moment, the Holy Spirit flowed between us. A new fire, a healing fire was melting away her fears, and instead of a torturous burning, a blessed warmth now wrapped itself around her. She closed her eyes; her shoulders sagged. Together we sat in silence for some time. It was too sacred to interrupt that healing space with something so trivial as words.

Incorporating a dying person's story into the story of Jesus's life, death and resurrection helps them begin to identify with God's passion, compassion and steadfast love for them. The hope of the good news becomes real. Death may not pale completely in the face of this revelation, but it loses some of its dread. The knowledge that we are a part of God's redemptive process *at this moment* is liberating. We stand outside of space and time, and death loses its sting. Our deliverance is secured by God's love and grace, even if we cannot comprehend quite what it will look like.

I had almost forgotten the prayer shawl I had brought with me. I had obtained several from the Episcopal Church of St. Michael and All Angels (Dallas, Texas) for use at the hospital. It was a beautiful crimson red, with a prayer card attached. I gently wrapped the shawl around her as I prayed with her. After the prayer, she grasped the shawl and snuggled deeply into it. "Oh," she breathed. "How beautiful. How lovely. Oh, you don't know how much good this has done me. I was so afraid before you came and now . . ." Her eyes were glistening with the faintest flicker of hope.

I left the woman's room with a profound sense of awe and humility, realizing that the importance of honest conversation at the end of life cannot be overestimated. She wanted reassurance that God loved her, that she was still human, despite her cancer and impending death. She was desperate for someone to listen to her unconditionally so that her deepest fears could be addressed, not laughed off or dismissed. And she wanted to be remembered not as a sinner beyond redeeming, but a woman worthy of heaven's eternal joy, reunited in a deeply spiritual way with her beloved husband at his future passing.

It's rare for such a profound spiritual breakthrough to happen so quickly. I often think of her, pondering whether her death was beautiful and peaceful with her renewed sense of self.

Palliare

As Dame Cicily Saunders, founder of St. Christopher's Hospice in London, states, "How people die remains in the memory of those who live on."[2] She remains in mine.

---

2. As quoted in *Your Life Talks*, "Dame Cicely Saunders—Pioneer of the Modern Hospice Movement," https://yourlifetalks.com/dame-cicely-saunders-pioneer-of-the-modern-hospice-movement/.

7

The Illusion of Control

THERE ARE MANY THINGS in life we cannot control. Death is one of them. It is inevitable that all human beings will face death. Of course, most people go to well-equipped hospitals when they are critically ill. And most people do get better. Modern medical technology and new wonder drugs now allow us to live longer, healthier lives. Many of us are living our days fully with titanium heart valves, hips, and shoulders, or with new bone marrow or transplanted organs. Why, the cure for cancer (and worse, old age!) might be just around the corner! It is easy to deny the reality of death when we can so easily forestall it. But progress does not mean that we will live forever. When death is imminent, a "good death" for the patient becomes a reality that is free from pain, suffering and uncertainty. According to an article in the *Journal of the American Medical Association*, patients facing death want a painless, peaceful exit, the presence of family, and the resolution of any financial or relational concerns.[1] A dying person does not want prolonged suffering. A dying person wants to know that his or her life has had meaning. One seeks peace with God, church,

---

1. Steinhauser et al., "Factors Considered Important," 2476–82.

The Illusion of Control

and self. They hope for "a sleep and a forgetting,"[2] and an assurance that they will reconnect with loved ones in the hereafter. He or she wants a measure of control throughout the dying process without loved ones being burdened with undue medical expenses and caregiving.[3] Ah, yes. Control.

Once I visited a patient who I'll call Mr. C. That was because he looked like the horror movie puppet "Son of Chucky." He was horribly maimed and scarred, stitches running back and forth across what was left of his neck like gruesome little train tracks. When I visited him, he had just awakened from surgery. His eyes were bright with pain and desperation. He could only moan. The only words I could understand were, "Hi," and "Kill me."

It did not have to be like that. He had most of his lower jaw removed due to head and neck cancer, not because he wanted it, but because his children wanted it. Sadly, his story is not unique. Mr. C had battled cancer for years. He never wanted to be in the hospital or mess with chemotherapy. His wife had done whatever her husband wanted and cared for him to the best of her ability, even when it meant diapering him and feeding him liquids through a syringe. She never got a good night's rest, because "When you're caring for someone you love, you're always listening for them, especially at night," she told me. Finally, they both talked things over. She needed help, and he did not want any heroic measures. They enrolled him in hospice. Doctors and nurses came several times a week, and he was content and pain-free in his own home.

But the couple's adult children were horrified with this decision. They believed that their mother was giving up on their father by using hospice care, that this was wrong, that everything should be done medically for him, despite the doctors telling them that surgery would only buy the patient some time. When the patient began to decline precipitously, they did not allow him the comfort of a peaceful passing. They converged around his bed, made a scene, pushed their mother out of the room, called an ambulance, and rushed their father to the hospital against his wishes. Then

2. Steinhauser et al., "Factors Considered Important," 2476–82.
3. Fine, "Achieving Excellence in Palliative Care."

they arranged for the patient to have a surgery that would not cure him, but instead extend his dying. Not once did the children acknowledge the patient's wishes. Because the children were hysterical, angry, forceful, and insistent, I doubt the patient's advance directives were ever even questioned by hospital personnel.

There was estrangement between the mother and children. My heart bled for her. Not once throughout my visit did the two sons present acknowledge that she was even in the room. They did not look at her or speak to her. They effectively blocked her way to the patient's bed, backs turned. Her husband kept looking around for her. She had to move to get into his range of vision. She smiled at him. He couldn't smile back, but he was comforted by seeing her. I am not a person who cries easily, but tears welled up in my eyes when I saw how these two looked at each other. This husband and wife had shared over fifty-five years together. They were young once, vibrant, and beautiful. He was devastated that "his girl" had to see him this way. And she was devastated that she had been overruled on a surgery that her husband hadn't wanted and that wouldn't stop his cancer. His tremendous suffering was being prolonged under the guise of "doing everything to keep him alive."

The patient was exhausted. Rest, however, was prevented by Son Number One hovering over him shouting, "Hey, there, Dad! You goin' to sleep? You're doin' great, Dad! The doctors say you'll be fine. Hey, Dad! Can ya talk to me? How ya feelin?" All this time, Poor Mr. C would start to doze off only to be startled awake by another question. "He's tired now," his wife said quietly, a remark that was completely ignored by both Son Number One and Son Number Two. This went on for a full half hour. "Hey Buddy! You feelin' sleepy? You wanna nap?" It was all I could do to not throat-punch these two idiots.

I have discovered that there are two sides to my brain. Not necessarily lobes or hemispheres. There is the sane part of my brain, and there is the other part, the part that's always trying to get me killed, fired, or in trouble. I knew that if I stayed and gave in to my anger, I would have made a scene. I would have forcibly yanked away both of those grown men from the patient's bed,

The Illusion of Control

called them some highly un-pastoral names and told them in no uncertain terms to get the hell out of that hospital room. But the nurses would have had to call security on me pronto had I done that, and thankfully, this time the sane part of my brain gained the upper hand. I turned to Mrs. C. and said quietly, "Do you have any questions for me?" "No, thank you. It's settled. He's going to a nursing home with hospice." Both sons shot her the stink-eye at the "H" word, while Mr. C again had that wild tragic look of despair. *Nursing home!* He never wanted this! He had wanted to pass peacefully at home in his own bed with his dear wife at his side!

Why, oh why, are we so afraid to let our loved ones die? Control. In the United States, nearly 76% of people die in an institutional health care setting. It has been my experience that health care providers are often the worst at helping patients and families deal with death. There are various reasons for this. Foremost is the focus on cure. No one comes to a hospital to die. Humans are hard wired to live and to fight for life. We come with the expectation we will get better. I have spoken with doctors who take it as a personal failure when a patient dies. When death will be the eventual outcome, health care providers may or may not communicate this in realistic terms to family members until the death is imminent.[4] This is truly shameful. Ecclesiastes tells us, "For everything there is a season, and a time for every matter under heaven; a time to be born and a time to die" (3:1–2) . . . "a generation comes and a generation goes" (1:4).[5] The preacher reminds us that we are mortal, as much as we want to believe that we are not. Eventually, we will all be faced with a terminal prognosis, a traumatic loss, or the impending death of a loved one. Here is where it is okay to say, "He or she has fought a good hard fight, but now it is time to let go and let God." This is neither denial nor fatalism. It is, perhaps, the best kind of control. The kind of control that allows for healing in all its forms.

---

4. Kubler-Ross, *On Death and Dying*.
5. Eccl 1:4; 3:1–2.

— *8* —

I'll Hold You Forever

Some years ago, one of my parishioners, Mr. M, died. He was a World War II veteran and a wonderful, caring man. He faithfully attended church with his wife, offered his home and heart to his own biological and adopted children, and was a gentle joy to be around. I never heard one angry or unpleasant word come from his mouth. Well, okay, he was a quiet guy overall. Still, even when he was most ill, he could laugh about how funny my husband acted (he played the comedian) in the church talent show.

When I first met him, Mr. M was suffering from the effects of congestive heart failure, which made it hard for him to breathe and sapped his energy. But nothing kept him from our little Episcopal church. Even when he was on a walker, he toddled along slowly, but happily, and insisted on making it up to the altar for communion. Then the day came when he could no longer make it to church. So, the church went to him. Wednesday was my day. I began to look forward to Wednesdays just so I could see his smile, feel his soft, warm hand in mine and pet his little dogs, who were never out of his lap. He showed me his World War II medals and his father's World War I medals. We shared a love of history, so we gabbled on about various battles and victories. I would share the news of the church with him and bring food. The church ladies *always* insisted

39

on my bringing him a plate from the Wednesday night church dinners. They all missed him, and food is a great comforter. And although Mr. M had no appetite, and Mrs. M was too keyed up to eat, they would graciously accept the meals "for tomorrow."

Each week we would take communion together. It was not my initial intention to include the dogs, but if you have puppies, you know they want to be included in everything. They would always jump up on my lap, licking, barking, and begging to be noticed. One time (although it wasn't intentional) I accidentally gave communion to the puppies. I had one dog on my lap, one at my feet, and the wafer in my hand. As I stretched the wafer out to my friend to partake, the lap dog intercepted with lightning speed, which caused the other dog to enter the fray, and both gulped it down. (Heck, *humans* should be so excited to receive communion!) Mr. M got such a kick out of it. He did not stop laughing until a coughing fit forced him to take some oxygen. After his breathing became better, I joked that I might be defrocked for such heresy as "giving" communion to dogs, but I figured this was an instance where compassion took precedence over liturgical correctness, and God's grace would intercede anyhow.

Mr. M finally grew too weak even for his walker. He sat in his recliner, as it was easier for him to breathe that way. And, as his heart was making more of an effort to keep pumping, he began experiencing pain and shortness of breath. He and his wife made the decision to enroll him in home hospice. There were no secrets, no denial, just a loving sharing of last days together. They both knew the truth. He was dying soon. So, they took joy in every moment together. They said things to each other they had never been able to say before. They prayed together. They loved on their dogs. The dogs knew death was coming. They just knew. They never left Mr. M's side. For four months, he lived securely in his own home, surrounded by his own things, in his own bed, with his puppies in his lap, and with his family around him. There were no tubes, wires, heart shocks, or pain. He had all the medicine he needed. His daughters came every day, making sure the house was decorated for Thanksgiving, then Christmas, then St. Patrick's

I'll Hold You Forever

Day and finally Easter. They all went through old photographs together, laughing, talking, and reminiscing. Mrs. M had a table in the hallway outside their bedroom that held old photographs. One was a picture of her husband as a small child. In another, he stood proudly in his wartime uniform. Yet another showed him handsome and smiling, tuxedo-clad, dancing with his daughter at her wedding. Mrs. M placed candles and a small Bible on the table, too, which caused some consternation from Mr. M. "But honey, this looks like an altar! I'm not dead yet!" he'd joke.

Gradually, my friend began sleeping more. He lost track of time, but it did not seem to bother him. He told me he knew it was Wednesday if I came, and it was Sunday if the rector visited. He was content to let his wife do most of the talking as she needed pastoral care as much or more than he did. One day, however, he did say that he knew he was going to die, and that he was not afraid. God had mercifully granted him that peace that took away the fear of the unknown.

Many people approaching imminent death within twenty-four to forty-eight hours or so experience terminal agitation. The body's organs begin shutting down and the neurotransmitters in the brain begin short-circuiting. Patients will suddenly display uncharacteristic energy. They will state an urge to go to the bathroom, kick off bedclothes, reject pats and hugs, or act irritated with loved ones' attempts to calm them. The morning Mr. M died he had been agitated like this. He was very disoriented and told his wife (who never left his side) that he needed to get to the bathroom. He tried to get himself out of bed and fell. His wife was immediately beside him, saying, "Don't worry, I'll hold you forever." She cradled him in her arms, put a pillow under his head, and covered him securely with a blanket. And that is how he died. Holy Sweet Jesus, can one hope for a better death? What could be better than being wrapped in loving arms, hearing, "Don't worry. I'll hold you forever." The absence of what he did not hear (noise, code status blared over the intercom, panic, fists pounding his chest, machines sending volts of electricity through him, utter chaos) was a blessing. As he slipped from earth to grasp the hands of Christ, I know that my friend heard a loving voice. "Don't worry. I'll hold you forever." In making our transitions, I pray we may all hear the divine voice whispering, "Don't worry. I'll hold you forever."

In the weeks following Mr. M's death, Mrs. M grieved and tried to become accustomed to that dreadful moniker, "Widow." Mr. M had been cremated, and about six weeks after the funeral, she picked up his ashes from the funeral home. She wanted them with her. She had looked for a lovely urn for them, but they cost upwards of five hundred dollars. She could not afford that, so the plain brown box took up residence on the hallway table with Mr. M's pictures and candles.

Then, while she was grieving her husband's loss, one of their little dogs also died. He was an old dog and lost without his master. He quickly grew so ill that the veterinarian gently told her she must put the animal down. Mrs. M went through the motions of taking the dog to the vet and held him as he passed, just as she had done with Mr. M. "Don't worry. I'll hold you forever." The dog had been so beloved, and the vet knew Mrs. M was going through a tremendous double loss. For don't we all love our fur babies as much as we do our human ones? He provided a handsome wooden case for the puppy's ashes, with a bronze nameplate. This box was given a place of honor next to Mr. M's ashes on the hallway table. Then Mrs. M sought solace in family, God, and church as she began the long journey of redefining her life.

A few weeks after the puppy's death, Mrs. M came back to our women's Bible study group. We all became tearful as she shared how hard it was to lose one's husband of fifty-plus years. We had all known and loved Mr. M and it was hard for us, too, to see only one of the well-known pair. Mrs. M shared with us, "Since B died, and then the puppy too, I've had the weirdest experience. Every time I would walk by B's ashes, I could swear I heard him say, 'Dammit, N!' This happened several times! I didn't know what to make of it! Every time I'd walk by that table, I'd hear his voice saying, 'Dammit, N!'" Mrs. M paused. She was not at all unnerved by this and accepted his voice from the other side as a matter of fact. "Well, I couldn't imagine why B would be so angry with me, so I went and sat by the table. And I asked him, 'B, Honey, what's the matter?' And do you know what he said?" "No!" our whole group breathed, on the edge of our seats. "He said, 'Dammit N! Even the *dog* has a nicer box than me! Is that the *best* you could do!?!'"

For a moment, there was absolute silence. Then, we all roared with laughter. It was twenty minutes before I could speak enough to restore any sort of order at all. "Well," I said, wiping my eyes, "then what did you do?" Mrs. M replied furtively, looking around almost like Mr. M was spying on her. "I looked at the puppy's box and it really was so much nicer than the plain old brown box they had B in, with no nameplate or anything. But I knew I could not afford the funeral home's expensive urns. So, I just called up the vet and asked him for a box for a *large* dog. It was only $50.00! And I had B's name engraved on it! And do you know what? I haven't heard B's voice since! So, I guess he's happy with what I did. Or maybe it's that he'll never forgive me!" More hysteria ensued. The whole thing was so funny, and yet so believable, we rejoiced in what had happened and thanked God for the mystery and craziness that is this earthly life.

God is so good to give us the gift of laughter to ease our pain! It is never wrong to allow humor in to heal our hurting hearts. It is not an affront to God or to the deceased if it is an experience of love, honor and compassion that grasps us like a warm hug and wraps us in tender memories. And it can remind us not to worry so much or fear what the future may bring. God's got us. Listen and see if you can hear him in the stillness, calming you, reassuring you and whispering, "Don't worry. I'll hold you forever."

9

Blindsided

A NEW PATIENT CAME into the intensive care unit one day. All the doctors were whispering about her. Miss G was a special case. Never seen anything like it, they said. No real studies or research on her condition. The patient was homeless, had no family, and had been a life-long crack addict. If that was not bad enough, this patient was suffering from a devastating reaction to a chemical that contaminates nearly 80% of the street crack currently sold in North America. It is *levamisole*. It is an anti-worming agent used in cattle, sheep, and pigs. It's also a filler that stretches cocaine, makes it cheaper to buy, and gives the user more bang for the buck. Unfortunately, levamisole is not meant to be used in humans. Usually, the adverse reaction is some dead skin on the earlobes, the cheeks or the nose. This woman's reaction was the worst anyone had ever seen. All of her skin, *all of it*, began to die. Your skin is your body's largest organ. When your skin dies, you die. Levamisole also causes problems with the body's white blood cells, leaving the patient with no way to fight off any infection. This patient was rotting literally from the outside in. She was grotesque, a sideshow exhibit from a carnival of lost souls.

Where her head should have been was a lumpy blackened blob. Gray-green gangrenous tissue had grown all over her face. It covered her eyes, and she was blind. There was no nose, and just a slash of mouth left. Her arms reminded me of molded beef jerky. Her fingers had fused together into useless flippers. She could not use them and was totally dependent on her medical team for all her bodily needs. The doctors removed the mirrors in her room on the off chance she might catch a blurry glimpse of herself. The rest of her body was paralyzed, and the dead skin was sloughing off in crusts which littered her white blanket like sooty black snow. The saintly ICU nurses took turns scraping off the necrotized tissue, gently putting soothing cream on the raw, pink wounds underneath. It was excruciatingly painful for the patient, and it traumatized the nurses to perform the process. It was a horrible thing to see, and to smell. Once you smell death, you never forget it. It's a sickly odor of decomposition that has a slightly sweet edge to it. The room reeked of it.

It was such a cruel, cruel way to die. And to die knowing you did this to yourself! I have seen ugly things in my twelve years of chaplaincy, including terrible burns, gunshot wounds, accident victims, gangrenous limbs, grotesque cancers, patients bleeding out. This was by far the worst. I took a deep breath, steeled myself and managed to enter the room. I sat by her bed. Even with a sterile gown, face mask and gloves, I dared not touch her. What do you say to a person like this, with no face and no future? "So, how's it going?" *Jesus Christ, puh-leeze!* Anything I had to say would sound totally inane. I really wanted to run screaming away from this gruesome apprehension. I lamely offered, "Miss G? It's Marci, the chaplain. How are you feeling today?" She whispered, "Blessed."

Blessed. Excuse me, what? Are you *kidding* me?

Earlier I described the two sides of my brain. The sane one vanished here. I began screaming inside of myself. "There is nothing blessed about this! Do you think God is blessing you now for making such poor choices in your life? Sleeping around on the streets with God-knows-who to get your next fix? You've lost everything! You look like a monster! You are dying a horrible death and you call yourself blessed?" Fortunately, Miss G was unaware of my judgmental inner rant.

Blindsided

I honestly did not know what to do. I was angry. I got angrier the longer I sat there. Angry that she had done this to herself. Angry that such a disgusting fate had been entirely preventable. Angry she was putting the nurses through a singular hell. Angry that poverty and ignorance had driven Miss G to this. Angry at all the other addicts out there who are lost in their own purgatories. Angry at drug dealers who sell death for their own profit. I have long since ceased to believe that God "causes" disease, "gives" people cancer, or "punishes" sinners for their shortcomings. We sinners do just fine in punishing ourselves, thank you very much. So, I wasn't angry at God. But how could she not be angry, or even express it? Of course, I couldn't read her facial expression. She had none. But she could still speak. There was not one shred of fear, anger, guilt, or desperation in her voice. Only a calm resignation.

Perhaps the crack had addled her brain to the point she was incompetent. Perhaps she just wanted to say what she thought the chaplain wanted to hear so I'd leave her alone. But perhaps it was I who didn't get it. Was she really that different from me? This woman had allowed her inner demons to take over her life, certainly. But I have inner demons, too. Too many of them. Legion. Ministers are easy prey for depression, drug addiction, alcoholism, and suicide, and its only by the smallest sliver of faith and God's amazing grace they have not taken me over. The only real difference between her and me was that I, as a white, educated, upper-middle-class woman had access to the best life has to offer—a fulfilling job, a nice home, good doctors, health insurance, supportive friends, and a loving family. I had *blessings. Real blessings,* right? But here's the thing. Her blessings were just different, that's all. She was not judging me. She did not seem angry at all that I had advantages and she did not. She quietly accepted me as part of her circle of caregivers and was grateful. Would I have had such an attitude if I were in her place? Doubtful. I would have resented the chaplain's white privilege and utter cluelessness about the gritty hell that is life under the overpasses in any given urban mix-master in America today. I would have refused to talk to anyone like me. I would be outraged at the unfairness of it all.

"Yes, I feel blessed," she repeated softly. "You all are taking good care of me. God is with me. I'm blessed." She held her flipper hand out to me, and I took it gently in mine. Somewhere, there was a wellspring of divinity inside of her crumbling body that assured her that the Lord was with her even as she was wasting away. There was hope, a hope I couldn't see. But she could. She had nothing but the cross of her spent body, her regrets, lessons learned too late and trust in a better life in the hereafter. But in this desolation, she found droplets of sweetness in the rock of her existence. Gratitude. *Real blessings.* She was the one who could not see, yet I was blindsided by her declaration of faith. I had been knocked off my assumptions like the apostle Paul on the road to Damascus and I was taken aback by this woman's simple love of God, the only thing she had left. Only when I took her brittle, crumbling hand in mine did the barrier of my own blindness break, allowing me to see her not as a monster but as God's beloved child, one whom he was empowering now, this moment, with strength and beauty. Most homeless people in the world die alone and forgotten. But not Miss G. I will remember her because of what she taught me; that I should look beyond the visible and have gratitude and acceptance for all God's *real* blessings, seen and unseen.

— 10 —

A *Pietà* in the NICU

When I attended seminary, I was assigned to serve my chaplain residency at a county hospital. It served the poor, the indigent, the disenfranchised, the mentally ill, the homeless. The doctors and nurses were highly regarded. The priests and chaplains serving the hospital even more so. Many of the patients who show up at the ER doors are minorities, undocumented immigrants and the uninsured. Most come with no prior medical care, especially pregnant women. Many poor mothers-to-be lack the funds for prenatal treatment, and fear either the general medical community, or deportation before their baby can be born. Many arrive at Labor and Delivery at a last resort, only when there are complications or birth is imminent. Unfortunately, some of these little souls don't have the chance to experience life on earth before they are lifted to a heavenly one.

One night, I was on call on the overnight shift. It was around 2:00 a.m. I was paged to Labor and Delivery. A patient had miscarried at twenty-three weeks. "Fetal demise." That's the sterile clinical term for a miscarriage or an infant death. I entered the room with some trepidation. This was my first experience with an infant death. I had been told that the mother was sixteen, was from El Salvador, that she didn't speak much English, and that

A Pietà in the NICU

she was very poor. I paused at the door a moment. How in the world was I going to relate to this woman, or her to me? I had two healthy babies and the perfect upper-middle-class White American life. What was I going to do?

I went in. The room was totally dark, except for the light filtering in from the hallway. I had trouble seeing the young woman in the darkness, but I could hear her. Great wrenching sobs that would melt a heart of stone. I sat down beside her. "Esposo?" She shook her head no. "Una madre? Un padre?" No. She was all alone. I sat with her for the longest time, in the dark, in a profound silence broken only by the young woman's wails. I thought of the passage from Jeremiah: "A voice is heard in Ramah, lamentation and bitter weeping, Rachel weeping for her children, she refuses to be comforted because they are no more."[1]

Finally, she turned and looked at me, tears streaming down her face. Her eyes were enormous, her face red and puffy. She pleaded in broken English. "Por favor, may I see mi nino? Mi nino. I want to see him. Just one more time? Bautismo, si? Por favor, Senora Capellana?"

What I really wanted to do was to run screaming out of that room. This was too painful! How in the world was I going to minister to this woman, to help her make sense of her premature child's death, something that seemed so senseless? I didn't have any answers. I didn't even speak her language! At that moment, God seemed very far away. So, I did what I usually do when I feel trapped. I had an internal argument with the divine.

"Why, Lord, have you taken this baby away now, here, on *my* shift? What have you done to me, God, bringing me out of my nice safe little seminary and plopping me here in this wilderness of heartache? I can't do this! I wish you'd let me alone! I don't want to be here in this terrible Ninevah! In fact, I'm striking out for Tarshish this very minute!" Before I could excuse myself, throw my hospital badge in the trash and call a cab, however, I felt God nudge. "Wait a minute. Don't be afraid." My dutiful response was, "Okay . . . God, did you not hear anything I just said? I'm lost here!

1. Jer 31:15.

Palliare

I can't baptize this baby; the baby's not alive! Oh, I can go through the motions, but it won't be a real sacrament, will it? I don't even know if she understands me!" God sighed a very long sigh. "Is this *really* all about you? Is it all about rules? Maybe you should attempt, just a bit, to understand her." "Okay, fine, God, just fine," I thought. "I'll stay. Send me a freakin' gourd I can sulk under."

The grieving young mother was mercifully unaware of my temporary insanity as I stretched out my hand to her. She clung to it as though it was a lifeline. "Bautismo?" "Si, si." I got my materials, a blessing ritual, and sacramental oil. I would not use water—I was too stubborn (oh, I'd show God!) and too locked into newly learned liturgical rules. I thought back to a recent seminary class in the rites of the church. Under no circumstances should you baptize a dead person. Baptism is one of the two most important Christian sacraments (the other being communion), ideally witnessed in community, with sponsors charged to assist the newly baptized in the ways of Christian living. But dead people are, well, DEAD. You can say a blessing or prayer over them, but it's up to God to do the rest. Funny how I seemed to forget that. That God would indeed do the rest.

The charge nurse brought in a tiny little bundle, wrapped in a blue blanket. She placed the bundle in the woman's arms. A hush fell over the room. For a moment, none of us even breathed. I have never seen such a look on anyone's face, and I may never again. Such love, such tenderness, such pride, such grief. A *Pietà* in a hospital bed. Does God look at us that way? She turned back the blanket from the baby's face and kissed the tiny head. I marveled at the perfect little head with its mop of black hair, the translucent skin, the miniscule fingers that looked like little wrinkled freshwater pearls. "He's beautiful," I whispered. "What is his name?" "Abraham. Mi nino es Abraham."

I anointed the child with oil, tracing the sign of the cross on a forehead still marked with the blood of birth. The mother's tears began again. They dripped from the mother's face onto the head of her son. And there! There was God's deliverance. The mother was baptizing the child with her tears.

Here was water from the fountain of a loving heart. "Out of the believer's heart shall flow rivers of living water" (John 7:38). Could anything be more sacramental? It didn't matter at all what I had done—what mattered was what God had done!

Thomas Hart writes, "Our spirituality would be much richer if we realized that . . . [the sacraments] are only some of the ways God meets us. If God is alive and well, interested in his world, and present to it at all times and places, if he is a God who is always disclosing himself and offering himself for relationship, then we may be in a communication situation much more than we usually imagine."[2]

And we were! When I anointed the child with oil, we affirmed the unity of Christ and the blessings of the Holy Spirit. When the mother bathed the child with her tears, the child was blessed and bound to both. I held both mother and child in my arms and the nurse and I took turns holding the baby ourselves, whispering coos and sweet little prayers. Abraham now was our baby too.

The nurse, myself, and the mother and child merged into a collective sisterhood where only life, hope and love mattered. Suddenly, there was no sense of rich or poor, cultural prejudice or comparative judgment. Instead, there was a sense of renewal. Yes, a tiny precious life was dead to this world, but certainly alive in the next. The presence of the Holy Spirit, God's *ruah*, was fully alive in that place where God's people were gathered, breathing a renewed sense of compassion, unity and power into the darkness of that hospital room.

---

2. Hart, "Art of Christian Living," 5.

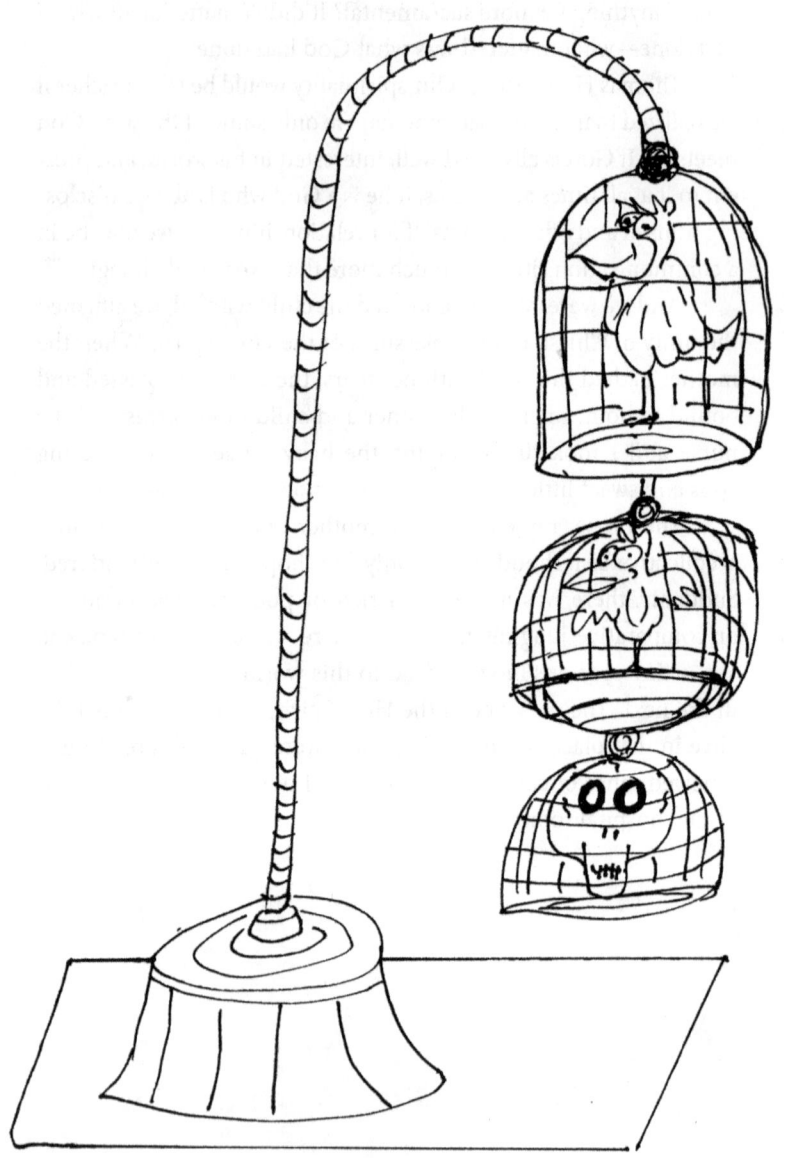

11

Broken Heart Syndrome

When I was a little girl, my grandmother Mimi would tell me of a dream she had shortly after her father died. He was in heaven. But he came to her in this dream, and they had a conversation. She asked him, "Daddy, are you happy?" He responded, "Marcia, you have no idea how happy I am." She begged him, "Won't you come back with us?" He said, "If you knew what it is like here, you wouldn't ask me to come back. I was sick there. I'm well here. You can't imagine how wonderful it is. I can do all the things I never could on earth. I can learn everything I couldn't learn there. See?" Then her Daddy gave her an amazing tour of the heavenly place where now he was. Mimi told me, "It was the most incredible thing I have ever seen! The colors were so vivid, much brighter and clearer than anything here on earth. There was a beautiful river and wide gold avenues and the trees lining the river were gold, with silver dripping from them. Daddy led me to a big stack of books, not like we have here, but like tablets emblazoned with all the knowledge of the universe. It was so beautiful. I wanted to stay with him, but he told me I had to go back and take care of my mother and sisters." Mimi would get tears in her eyes telling me this story, but of course I wanted to hear it again and again.

I loved Mimi's story of heaven. I thought how beautiful it would be to go there. But when you are young and healthy, you can't conceive of dying. Heaven is a mythical fairy tale place run by a large, bearded Anglo-Saxon guy that looks a lot like Santa Claus, except he's not so chubby and he's wearing white, not red. There are angels floating around on wispy clouds and you imagine it might be nice to end up there. But later. Like decades later. As a child, I certainly could not understand dying, much less someone *wanting* to die. Now I do. Because now I know something about unresolved grief.

Unresolved grief kills. Studies have shown that unresolved grief can cause very real physical symptoms and that repressed emotions in response to a death will manifest later in unhealthy ways, including depression, anxiety, high blood pressure, insomnia and even an increased risk of immuno-suppression leading to heart disease and certain types of cancer.[1] To go even farther, physicians today are beginning to recognize a condition they call "broken heart syndrome." It sometimes goes along with the catch-all diagnosis "failure to thrive," but it is much more complicated. Broken heart syndrome usually follows the loss of a spouse of many years or another tragic loss from which the patient cannot recover. But many years before I became a chaplain, I knew about broken heart syndrome. When I was a young college student at the University of Louisville in 1983, my grandparents, whom I adored, died within a week of each other. They had both suffered from various medical issues, but they came from an era that equated going to the hospital with certain death. They only trusted their chiropractor, who was a personal family friend, and that nice young podiatrist down the street who flirted with my Mimi something awful and made her laugh. Getting your neck adjusted or your thick diabetic toenails clipped was okay, but hospitalists and general physicians were to be avoided at all costs. *Because they were sure to find something wrong with you.*

Sure enough, they did. In her late sixties, Mimi was diagnosed with Type II Diabetes, congestive heart failure, and hypertension.

---

1. Balk et al., *Handbook of Thanatology*, 62.

Broken Heart Syndrome

Did she go to the hospital for care? Of course not! She jokingly denied she had anything at all wrong with her and continued to chain smoke Pall Malls and indulge in her favorite orange wafer cookies, happily dipping them in a big jar of marshmallow fluff. I am not making this up. That was Mimi.

Mimi suffered from incontinence, and laughed this off too, giggling to cover up the pain of her embarrassment. My grandfather Howard put a plastic cover down in the car because of her many accidents in it. I still remember that car. A 1968 maroon Chevy Impala with wide pleather covered seats. The seat cover didn't do much good though. The car smelled so strongly of urine that Howard had to drive with the windows down and the air conditioner or heater going full blast, depending on the time of year. I don't think he ever said a complaining word to Mimi about it, though. He adored her too much to embarrass her further. All this time, my grandmother refused to discuss their worsening health. She did her best to keep things hidden from my family. We found out about her copious nosebleeds only when she called us to say she was fresh out of clean towels, and could I bring some over, and I discovered she was suffering excruciating gall bladder attacks when she showed me a three-inch blister on her stomach caused by a heating pad. Why this alone didn't kill her, I don't know. Again, this was "nothing," and she was "fine." Of course, she was not fine. Within the year, it became obvious that both Mimi and Howard were declining. But nothing could convince them to go to the doctor for any kind of treatment. They clung to every last bit of independence they could grasp. When Howard finally collapsed at home and was taken to the hospital, he was diagnosed with lung cancer that had metastasized to his brain. There was nothing medically to be done. Within two months he was dead. Mimi would not go to the hospital to see him. She could not bring herself to watch him die. When we returned home from our sad vigil, we told her of her husband's death. Mimi closed her eyes, went into her bedroom, and shut the door. We didn't interrupt her. We respected her time of private grief. I am convinced during that time she talked to her beloved and pledged she would join him in heaven as soon as she could. After all, she knew what heaven was like. I also believe that because Howard loved her so much, his soul hovered, lingering near her to comfort and sustain her. I truly feel that loving souls do this for a while after the body passes. They want to make sure we are ok. Three days later, Mimi quietly suffered a stroke and died. She was afraid of living without her beloved husband, her little house, her cats, her precious knick-knacks, and pictures of her grandchildren. She was not afraid to die.

You know, though, it is not always the loss of a dear one that defeats us. My mother died within eighteen months of downsizing to a condo. Really. Mom suffered from a particularly virulent form of rheumatoid arthritis, and as she aged, it became too hard for her to brush her hair, drive her car, or even fasten her bra, much less clean her large home. My father initiated the move to a senior condominium community. He loved it; no more yard work for him! But after they moved, Mom became horribly depressed. She felt as if she were living in a strange hotel. There were no beloved neighbors waving to her from across the yard, and she refused to meet any new ones. She was no longer the matriarch and hostess of a grand house. She no longer had any real independence. When she could no longer cook because she couldn't lift or hold the pans, she gave up trying to adjust to her new "normal." When she developed stomach pains, she waved it off as "something I ate." One month later, her intestine ruptured and she died of sepsis. That's what the doctors said, anyway. But I know in the depths of my soul she really died of a broken heart, too bereaved at the loss of her younger, independent, active self to go on.

Bereavement is the psycho-social-emotional-spiritual experience of loss. There are varying degrees of loss, of course, and most people find that they can cope with the experience. Often, however, grief is not something we can overcome once and for all.[2] Rather, it is a process that may be resolved, but only after the grief itself has been addressed "with an understanding that aspects of it are never gone permanently or totally in cases of major loss, and that the loss has been accommodated and integrated appropriately

---

2. Rando, *How To Go on Living*, 225.

Broken Heart Syndrome

into the rest of one's life."[3] My grandmother and my mother were not able to do this. I do not blame them for it. They simply did not have the will nor the desire to struggle or to move forward with their respective griefs. They were just too sick and tired. When a heart is truly broken, the person cannot see how their suffering and grief can ever be resolved. The heart cannot be mended without some heavy-duty grief work and a reliance on God and others to help. Most people do find ways to work through their losses and their heartbreaks. Sometimes, though, we just can't. And it's okay. Because God welcomes the most broken kinds of people into his kingdom. He doesn't blame us for being shattered, whatever the cause. He doesn't condemn us for not having enough faith, or for not relying on him more, or for making poor choices, or even for taking our own lives because sometimes mental illness, desperation and hopelessness are just too much for us to handle. If he did, he wouldn't be a God worthy of our worship. Instead, God takes the snapped and splintered shards of our lives and mends them like an expert potter into something better, more eternal. Whole. This is heaven. We will experience it one day. The truth is, we all are cracked eikons[4] in need of healing. Even if there is nothing left of our life but shattered pieces crying out for restoration, we are still God's creation *in his image*.[5] We are still God's beloved, receptive to love and forgiveness. Our hope is that we will be restored by our loving Creator, "seeing the glory of the Lord as though reflected in a mirror, transformed into the same image from one degree of glory to another."[6] We will at last be whole.

---

3. Rando, *How To Go on Living*, 225.
4. McKnight, *Community Called Atonement*.
5. *Dictionary.com*, "Icon," http://dictionary.reference.com/browse/icon.
6. 2 Cor 3:18.

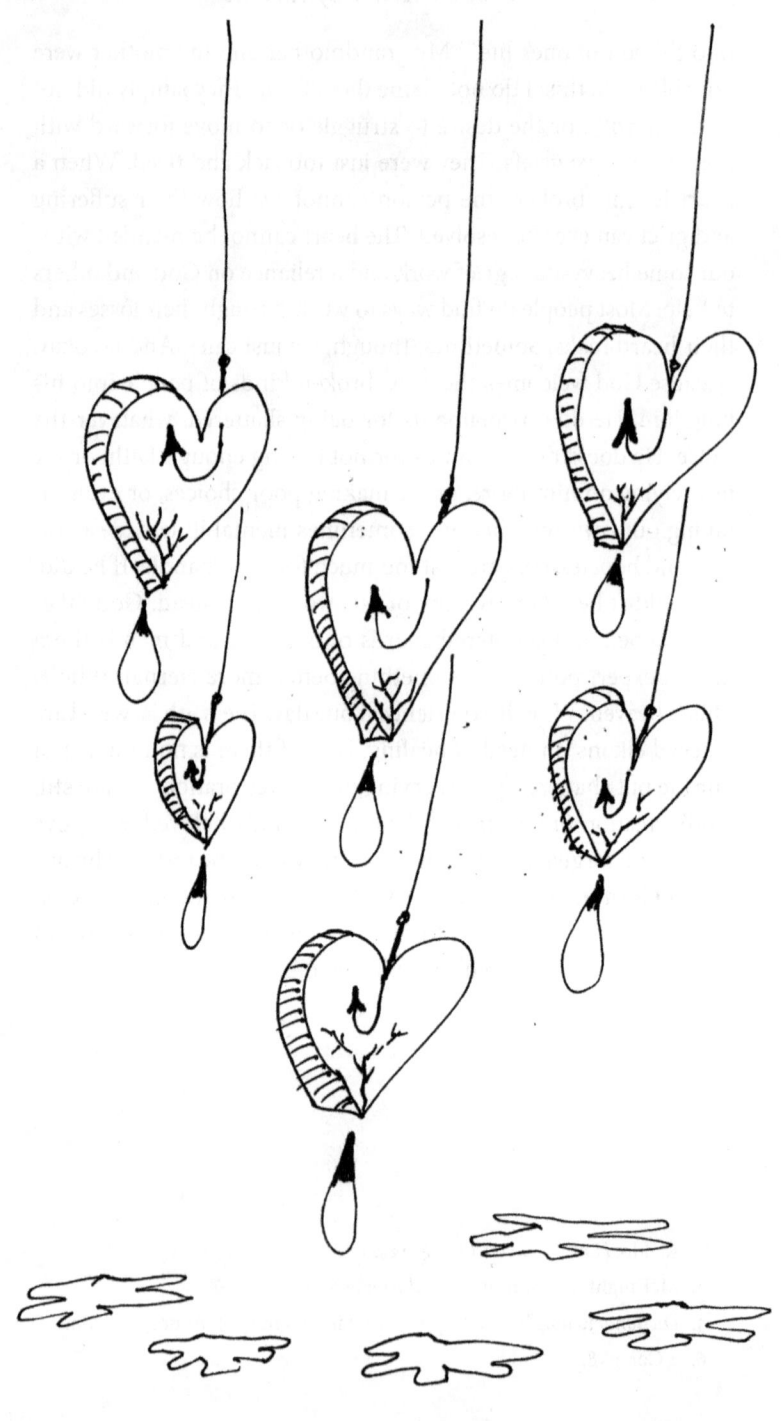

— 12 —

Jagged Little Secrets

When I was an assistant priest in a North Texas parish, I had a parishioner, Mrs. J, whom I visited in her at her home. She lived comfortably on a quiet tree-lined street near the church with her husband in retirement. They had no children. They didn't associate with many people. I knew Mrs. J suffered from some anxiety, and that her husband had some slight cognitive impairment, but by all appearances, everything seemed normal. One day after church, I found Mrs. J sitting alone at one of the parish hall tables. Everyone else had left and I was gathering my things and getting ready to lock up. Mrs. J had a cup of coffee in front of her, but she wasn't drinking it. She looked like she was going to faint. She was trembling and perspiring. She held out her hand to me. "Oh, Mother Marci! I'm so glad to see you! I need a little help." She looked very pale. "Mrs. J! Are you ok? What's wrong?" I feared she might be having a heart attack. "I just need, I just need . . . Can you look in my purse? My pain pills." I rummaged through her purse and found a bottle of hydrocodone. She took a couple and gulped her coffee. Within a few minutes, she seemed better. I had not been aware that Mrs. J needed pain pills for anything, and when I asked her about it, Mrs. J brushed off my concerns and assured me she was perfectly able to drive home, that she had just had a "sinking spell." I followed her home, just to make sure.

I usually visited Mrs. J once a month on Thursday afternoons, and at my next scheduled visit, she seemed unusually drowsy. "I can't seem to sleep anymore. So, I have a little wine. Take a sleeping pill. Watch television. You know, there's nothing worse than insomnia." We talked together and prayed as we usually did. During our prayer, Mrs. J dozed off. Mr. J ushered me out, stating she'd had a stomach ache the night before and he hoped she could get some rest.

The next time Mrs. J came to church, she fell asleep in her pew. Quietly, the ushers got her up and took her into the Bride's Room where there was a couch. It wasn't long before she woke up and blamed her drowsiness on not sleeping (again). She joked she'd been watching an old movie until the wee hours. "You know, Cary Grant is my favorite. I just can't help myself." I scolded her, "He's my favorite too, but not on Saturday nights with church in the morning! No more chardonnay matinees for *you*! Please take better care of yourself, Mrs. J." For a time, there were no more incidents and the red flags I was observing dipped to half-staff.

I was leading a Bible study one afternoon when we all heard a tremendous crash outside. We dashed out to discover that Mrs. J had run up over the curb in the parking lot and crashed her Buick sedan into a light pole. Praise God, no one was hurt. She was shaken and crying, and she apologized repeatedly. "Oh, I'm so sorry. I'm so sorry! I don't know how this happened!" I took her into the church office to wait for the tow truck. "Mrs. J, I'm really, really worried about you. You don't seem well lately. What is happening?" "Nothing. I'm just not sleeping very well, and it makes me a little dizzy sometimes." I decided to broach my concerns. "Mrs. J, I know you take pain pills. Is there any chance they could be making you dizzy or interacting with other medications?" She went from pitiful to defensive in a flash. "Of course not! I don't take anything that isn't prescribed specifically for me. I appreciate your concern but I'm fine."

During the next few months, everyone could tell something was not right with the J's. My monthly visits were postponed. Mr.

J would call me and cancel, saying Mrs. J was too tired, had another appointment, was out of town or she "just wasn't up to it." One Sunday she showed up at church with a black eye. "Silly me, I tripped over the garden hose. I'm just so clumsy!" I approached Mr. J alone to see if I could find out more. "She's just tired," he assured me. "Low blood sugar probably the culprit. She's been to the doctor. She's ok." "Can we do anything to help?" I asked. "Oh nothing, thank you, Mother. We don't need any help."

Gradually, the J's stopped coming to church altogether. My attempts at visiting them were rebuffed. Phone calls went unanswered. The red flags were flying at full staff again. I suspected polypharmacy.

Polypharmacy, the taking of multiple medications, is a huge problem in our society. Seniors are especially vulnerable to slick advertising campaigns that promise everything from better digestion to better sex. And some people cannot deal with the normal processes of aging. While no one wants to suffer wrinkles, arthritis pain, cracking joints, or a waning libido (especially a waning libido!) it's all too easy to become terrified of suffering anything at all. Television commercials play into our psyche that we all should be eternally young, thin, healthy, sexy, and beautiful. If a pill can fix it, why not get one? Or two? Or more?

I was ready to initiate a welfare check when I received a frantic call from Mrs. J's neighbor. She had gone over to check on the couple and found Mrs. J unconscious on the floor and Mr. J sitting beside her, dazed. "I can't wake her up and I don't know how long she's been down. I've called 9-1-1. Can you come right now, please?" When I arrived, Mrs. J was lying on the floor beside the bed. Mr. J had put a pillow under her head and a blanket over her. An uneaten cup of pudding lay next to her. Mr. J looked at me like he was in a dream. "She's been like this since last night. I tried to get her to eat. I kept thinking she'd get back up. I tried, but I can't lift her. I didn't know what to do," he said. Mrs. J was still breathing and had a pulse, but her mouth drooped slightly. *Sweet Jesus, what is going on here? Why didn't you call someone, Mr. J!*

When the paramedics arrived, they immediately began their examination. "Does she take any medications?" Mr. J hesitated.

Then he sighed and pushed open the bathroom door. The paramedic and I looked in. We both whispered, "Oh my God." Inside that bathroom were hundreds of pill bottles. They covered the toilet tank, the countertop and even the rim of the bathtub. Hidden in the depths of the medicine cabinet, the paramedic discovered more than eight hundred Neurontins. Sleeping pills. Valium. Pills for high blood pressure, cholesterol, arthritis, hypothyroid, antacids, pain. All prescribed by different doctors. Picked up at different pharmacies. Suddenly, I knew why Mr. J didn't call anyone. Mrs. J was an addict. And he didn't want anyone to know.

While the paramedics were taking care of Mrs. J, I sat down with Mr. J and took his hand. He was crying softly. "Mr. J, why didn't you tell me? Why didn't you let us help you?" Sadly, he told me their story. His wife had suffered from anxiety and insomnia for forty years. She had been able to manage it. But in recent years, things had changed. She would panic if she could not get her pills. And she needed more. For sleep, for calm, for pain, for whatever she imagined was wrong with her. When her anxiety became too much, she would beg to go to whatever physician she thought would help her. She would become hysterical if opposed. She would ask for more medicine or different medicine, because, as she claimed, the other meds weren't working, and she *needed* it. Her physicians would acquiesce for a time, but finally would realize she was abusing her prescription drugs, she had developed a tolerance, and they would stop prescribing them. When this happened, she angrily stormed out of their office threatening to sue. She would find other doctors. She would lie about her past medical history. And they would prescribe more pills, whatever would get this problematic patient out of their office.

Mr. J also gave up trying to fight with her. If he had to go to a twenty-four-hour pharmacy, he would go at 3:00 a.m. to get his wife what she wanted. He learned to just keep pills handy and an open bottle of wine around to wash them down. Whatever kept the peace and kept her happy. He was too exhausted to do anything but comply. The only rest he got was when she passed out asleep. He was ashamed of her addiction, and he had done his best to hide it. Sadly,

I thought of chats where he had brushed off her slurred speech and her absences at church, attributing them to low blood sugar, a bad night, food poisoning, or whatever other excuse he could think up. Unfortunately, Mrs. J had suffered a massive stroke. I wish I had intervened sooner. But honestly, I don't know if it would have helped because pastors must respect boundaries and people must ask for (and want and be willing to act upon) help for themselves. The Js hid her addiction from everyone up until the last, her dirty little secret locked up behind the bathroom door. Theirs was a generation that did not talk about such problems because of the stigma that would result if "we didn't just keep this to ourselves." Oh, how I wish for the love of God that one of them had spoken up!

The Episcopal Book of Common Prayer contains a prayer called, "For the Sanctification of Illness" (BCP 460).[1] For years, I have been fascinated with this prayer and the idea that illness, of any kind, including addiction, can become sanctified. Notice that I did not say "cured." True addiction and the accompanying psychosis and dependence that comes with it needs immediate professional help. I cannot emphasize that enough. Not all illnesses can be "prayed away." But a certain amount of suffering can be a holy thing if we are able to stop denying the existence of our deep existential pain and, through it, draw closer to God and find appropriate help. Jesus embraces our weakness and draws it up onto the cross with him. If we give him our burdens, he will carry them when we are too ill, mentally, and physically, to do so.

I still visit Mrs. J. She knows I am a nice person, and she smiles at me. But the damage to her brain has limited her speech. She is no longer anxious. She is no longer panicked about anything. She sleeps most of the time. And I suppose that is a blessing, in a sad, warped kind of way. Jesus is carrying Mrs. J in his arms, I am certain, and she finally has the peace that she was unable to experience for so many years. She has been sanctified through God's infinite mercy, even though she was not strong enough to bring herself to the foot of the cross first.

---

1. *Book of Common Prayer*, 340.

— 13 —

Sex and the Senior

You had to have known my dad.

Most of my memories of Dad have to do with his love of beer, his wonderful garden in our lush Kentucky backyard, his loud, ear-splitting laughter and his corny sense of humor. He would give you the shirt off his back, and if you needed something fixed, he was your go-to man. He had a marvelous gift for mechanics and was always puttering with the cars, the wiring, the plumbing, or whatever else needed repair. Sometimes he'd break things just to fix them. I have vivid memories of him down in the basement on a ladder, banging a hammer into the ceiling to stop the kitchen floor above from squeaking. My poor mother had to stand on the kitchen floor in the spot Dad marked and rock back and forth so Dad could pinpoint where the nail should go. If you have ever had to do this, it is bone-jarring. When Dad would start banging, Mom would start yelling. "*Jesus*, Country (his nickname) that nail just went through my foot! I'm going to get lockjaw!" He'd yell back up the stairs, "Aw, Annie, you've just got Hybuchetempomoco of the Blowhole!" Yep. Fun times. In case you are wondering, "Hybuchetempomoco of the Blowhole" is an imaginary illness invented by my family. Anytime anyone had any kind of ailment, they had

"Hybuchetempomoco of the Blowhole." Why? Because it's fun to say, it made the sufferer laugh, and my family was weird.

My father was an extremely virile, energetic, handsome man. After my parents moved to their senior community, and Mom died, the widows there circled around Dad like drooling vultures. Mom was not even cold in her grave before they started dropping off casseroles and leaving notes inviting him on dates. One note actually read, "Dear Larry, I'm five foot two and I have a hot tub. Meet me at 7:00 p.m." God's. Honest. Truth.

Dad was very lonely and lost after Mom died. They had been married for fifty-seven years. The only thing he knew how to cook were fried egg and bacon sandwiches. He had never lived on his own and he truly grieved the loss of my mother. He had adored her despite the fact they had a troubled marriage. Without her, he wandered around like a little lost puppy. Until he met G.

I found out about G when she called my house in Dallas to talk to Dad. Mom had been gone about six months and Dad was visiting my family and me in Texas. When she introduced herself, "Hi, It's G! Can I speak to Larry?" I blurted out, "G *who*?" "Your dad's friend, G." *Uh huh*. I shot Dad a sideways glance and handed him the phone. Dad sheepishly went into the other room. When he came back into the living room after the call, he looked so guilty. "Dad, have you got a girlfriend?" "Yeah. I met her on a blind date our friends set up." He was looking at me tentatively for approval. "Oh, for heaven's sake, Dad, you're eighty-three years old! You don't need my approval; you can do whatever the hell you want!" Fortunately, my siblings and I were not the types to tell Dad he could not live his life the way he wanted. True, it was not long after Mother's death, but Dad really seemed to like this lady. He seemed *happy* for the first time in a long time. If it was a mistake, it was his to make.

Several months later, I traveled to Dad's hometown to meet G. To my great relief, she was a delight. She was a devout Catholic, a widow with five children, a wonderful cook, and she doted on my father. I noticed that there was all new furniture in Dad's bedroom. Dad brushed it off by saying it was old and broken and he just wanted something new. I was a bit disappointed, as it was Mother's antique mahogany bed set. She had been born in that four-poster and I had wanted it for sentimental reasons. But it was Dad's to do with as he pleased. Too late now, anyway.

When G and Dad got married, my family gave them our blessing. We threw a big celebration to meet her family and I can honestly say they were all wonderful. I looked forward to getting to know them better. Everyone was happy that Dad and G had found each other. But life is not always kind. Three months later, Dad began to have trouble breathing and experiencing weakness in his legs. He was diagnosed with acute interstitial fibrosis, a disease that turns the lungs into scar tissue. It was terminal. Dad did all right for a few months. Then he declined rapidly, was placed on palliative care, and died peacefully with G, my brother and I at his bedside.

The week after Dad's death, I stayed at their condominium with G to plan the funeral. It was a crash course in grief counseling for me. G could not rest. We would walk in the nearby park for hours, talking about Dad's life, his childhood, his war service, my mom. One night, she cracked open a large bottle of wine, crying and reminiscing. "We wanted to do so much! We wanted to travel, to visit you in Dallas, to just be together," she sobbed. I comforted her as best I could. I'm just so glad you were together for the time you had. You took such good care of him, G. I was very happy for you both." I cried too and poured another glass of wine. By now, we were both a bit sloshed. I raised my glass in a toast and I ventured, "G, my dad was eighty-four and you're sixty-eight. I just hope that your relationship with him was, well, was . . ." *Here I paused, wondering the best and most discreet way to put the obvious.* "As close as it could be." She raised her glass, "Oh Honey, he was the best sex I ever had!"

For those of you who are shocked at this, *get over it.* Your parents had sex. You are proof of that. Stop being put off by the fact that Grandma might want a little hanky-panky now and then. Sex is not a timecard that life hands you in your teens only to tell you to clock out at age sixty-five. Just because one is of a certain age doesn't mean one's interest in intimacy magically evaporates.

As proof of this, I once witnessed a fist fight break out in a senior community hallway between two women who were duking it out over a frail, ugly little old man sitting nearby who looked as if he might blow himself away with a good sneeze.

After G's confession, I started giggling. Then outright guffawing. "*Holy Shit!*" I fell off the couch and leaned against it on the floor, pouring more wine and laughing until I almost snorted it out of my nose. G laughed too and went on. "I don't know quite how it happened, but one day we just started kissing and then fell into bed together. That was the start of our sexual relationship. It was before I called you that first time. Honey, I've never had such great sex! He never used Viagra and told me if he ever did take it, *he would kill someone!* (Here I just laid out on the floor, hysterical). We broke the bed in his room and had to get another one. And the next-door neighbors started to complain!" So *that* was what happened to Mother's bed! *Yippee ki yay, motherfuckers!*[1] At least it went out for a good cause! Take *that*, you Jealous Vulture Widows!

We laughed so much that night. It was wonderful to know my father had intimacy and happiness during the last year of his life. My husband has often said that he hopes he will be able to break a bed when he's eighty-four. I'm not sure I share his sentiment. Ow! But then, you had to have known my dad. Let's just say it's a blessing to go out with all your faculties. Can I get an amen?

---

1. McTierman, *Die Hard*.

14

Communion, Disinfected

COVID-19 SUCKS. I AM a homebody and love quiet time spent at home reading, writing, doing yoga, and walking alone through my neighborhood. I needed a vacation from church, and I enjoyed the COVID-19 quarantine for a while. At first. But then the quiet became eerie. A government enforced lockdown closed businesses, schools, day cares, restaurants, beauty salons, and movie theaters. Restaurants closed. Many have not reopened, and some have gone out of business. Grocery stores have reopened, but the shortages! Who would have ever thought we see shortages of toilet paper, isopropyl alcohol, baby wipes, bread, and pasta? Empty shelves in prosperous, selfish, wasteful America! In some stores I frequent, flour and canning supplies are still in short supply. Because stuck at home, people are making bread and canning again. That's not such a bad thing, I guess, except for the inconvenience.

Wearing masks sucks. It's not because of any political vendetta about my personal freedoms being taken away. It's because masks are impersonal, hot, and uncomfortable. Masks mess up my make-up. And, if I eat Italian food, I must deal with my own garlic breath. Ick. But masks save lives, so I wear one. If I can prevent someone (or myself) from getting sick, it's worth it and I will deal with it. Like a grownup. Vaccines, on the other hand, don't suck. What a miracle that vaccines were produced in time to save thousands of lives! What *does* suck is that people remain suspicious of them.

Isolation sucks. We are all isolated to some degree while this pandemic remains a threat to society. But it's especially tragic for seniors because isolation can be more lethal in some ways than the coronavirus itself. Why? Because when family members and friends are prevented from visiting in person, the patient cannot benefit from the gift of human touch and emotional support. Nursing staff, especially at night, also may decrease. Non-essential personnel, such as chaplains, are not allowed to assist with socialization. A patient with dementia previously interacting with others and enjoying activities can become confused and anxious when loved ones merely wave through a facility window but do not come in for a personal visit. "Don't you love me anymore? Why don't you come in?" Without personal engagement, people withdraw.

I remember one sweet couple I visited at a care facility prior to the pandemic. The husband was admitted to hospice for congestive heart failure and was doing well, considering. But then the virus turned into a pandemic and the facility went into lockdown. His wife of over forty years was denied personal visits. The couple talked on the telephone together several times a day. She would come to the hospice facility and wave at him through his window. But it wasn't the same. Inevitably he became lonely and anxious. He declined quickly and suffered a heart attack. Then, in a tragedy that should not have happened, the facility did not let his wife in to be with him as he died. When I placed a condolence call to her, the poor woman sobbed, "I didn't even get to hold him! I couldn't be there to tell him I loved him! What if he died thinking he was all alone? How am I supposed to live with this guilt?" How could I comfort her? I babbled off something about how no one has control over the pandemic and ever-changing government mandates. I felt like a parent in a Peanuts movie, where everything an unseen adult says to Charlie Brown or Linus sounds like it is coming from underwater. Meaningless sounds that communicate little or nothing. Countless other families are heartbroken and riddled with guilt because the same thing has happened to them. And damn it, there is not much we can do. Tele-health and Zoom meetings just are not the same as being able to hold your loved one as they pass.

Isolation leads to mental, physical, and emotional decline. Human beings are not meant to live in isolation. We thrive in community. "Normal" ways of being in community and being present to others in society have been decimated. Take, for instance, church. Virtual Communion (via video, Facebook Live, Zoom, or YouTube) bind us together, yes, but in a different way. I'm too much of a lover of all things liturgical to say it is *the same* as attending church in person. It is not the same. When churches were closed for months due to the virus, it added to our isolation not only as inherent beings of humanity, but also as members of our respective church communities. Not attending church made many of us lonely and anxious.

I'm an Episcopal priest. During the worst of the pandemic crisis, I hated the fact that I could not hold the Host, then pass it from my hands to those of a parishioner at the altar. No common cup, either. Communion wafers were relegated to little zip-lock bags in a basket by the door so that parishioners could take at least one form of the Eucharist with them on their way out. Some churches scheduled specific times for drive-by communion. "Hey, everyone! Come get your own special communion baggie in the church parking lot!" (Everyone wearing a mask, of course.) For a while choral singing was prohibited. No coffee hour. No hugging dear friends. No passing of the peace unless you were observing social distancing via a royal wave of the hand. Church attendance, when permitted again, prohibited people from sitting within six feet of each other in specially marked spots. That of course limited the number of worshippers allowed in. Our holy pas-de-deux was reduced to a bland solo. Disinfected Eucharist. Communion scrubbed within an inch of its life. And oh, how I hated it!

Because the Jesus I know got his hands dirty. He broke unsterilized bread. He drank from a cup soiled with the lips of sinners. He spat, made mud with his saliva, and rubbed it on the blind to restore sight. He touched raw, open wounds and bleeding women. Our belief in the saving power of Jesus calls us to "do this in remembrance of me." Orthodox Christians like me never fail to love the sense of wonder and awe that comes with kneeling at

Communion, Disinfected

the altar and partaking of the mystery of Jesus's body and blood. Unsanitized. Like the Crucifixion, our salvation is offered to us in all its sacred, dirty, bloody, shared glory.

Of course, I knew why priests and pastors had to go to such extremes. We had to keep our churches alive and keep our parishioners alive. We clergy did as we were instructed by our bishops, our church leaders, our government leaders, and the Centers for Disease Control. We still do. The church's experience during the pandemic has reminded me of that heartbroken wife standing on the outside of the care facility, looking in, desperately wanting to hold her dying husband. We want to hold each other. We long for sacred touch. When we are relegated to tele-religion, it hurts our hearts that we cannot come inside God's house to spend time with Christ and with each other. Watching worship on one's living room television or laptop just doesn't cut it for me. But many of us have settled for this due to health reasons, an ongoing fear, or merely the current rise in acceptability of online church.

Unfortunately, I am not sure that the traditional church as we know it will ever recover the numbers or the personal involvement we saw pre-COVID. When I look at the crucifix hanging in my office, I wonder if the church, like the dying Jesus, is being bled of its traditional relevance and meaning. I pray that the Holy Spirit, that most holy Advocate, will resurrect it. We are all desperate for that time when the COVID viruses will be a distant memory. Until then, some of us remain on the outside looking in. We place our hand on a stained-glass window, waiting for another to see us and press back.

Ultimately, there is still the comfort of hearing the prayers, a lone voice lifting a well-known hymn, and the service of the Word. There is still the holiness of the confession, and the joy of the absolution. There is still the mystery of the Word made flesh. There is still something about those little clean wafers in the little clean baggies that will always transcend our efforts to sterilize them. Even if we are just watching others partake on YouTube, we are brought into the holy anyway. We are engaged in communion anyway, and God himself consecrates us anyway, even if it looks and feels vastly different from times past.

— 15 —

All I Want is World Peace and a Pedicure

"All I Want is World Peace and a Pedicure." The sign was hanging above my spa chair in a North Dallas nail salon. I chuckled to myself at such a clever marketing banner as I settled in and placed my feet in the swirling tub of warm water. World peace is out of my league, but a pedicure I can do. A pedicure, I've found, can cure a lot of ills.

I started retreating to the nail salon when I became a hospital chaplain. My specialty was palliative care and hospice. For ten years, I dealt with horrible situations, terminal diseases, and death on a daily basis. At the end of a particularly draining day, I could escape to the one place I knew no one would ask anything of me, except payment for services rendered. Just the smell of a little acetone, and the clouds would begin to lift.

I've frequented numerous nail salons over the years (there's one on every street corner in Dallas). I've been to upscale salons that market all kinds of aesthetic spa services and cheap hole-in-the-wall places that smelled of garlic and pho and which I entered against my better judgment. But the need for escape is sometimes so strong that it's either that or get in my car and just keep driving until the land stops. It's therapy and it's cheaper than a Ferrari.

Time spent sitting in the pedicure chair has not been wasted. It's relaxing, and life makes more sense to me when I'm relaxed. But it's more than that. Somehow, I become much more in tune with my surroundings. Rather than shut down, my senses become much more acute. Smell becomes sharper, hearing blends into a cacophony. Touch feels like a divine blessing. I ponder how I might cultivate peace within my world, especially now that I am an Episcopal priest. What might I learn that can help others needing the same solace? I meditate within my soul as slender dark-haired doves flutter gently around me, feeding my hunger to be touched without any expectation of return and without a hint of existential guilt.

Services in beauty salons involve a plethora of touch. This is the main reason I go. I love being touched solely for hedonistic relaxation. Take foot rubs, for instance. I practically slip into unconsciousness when someone rubs my feet. I've given up asking my husband for foot rubs because he complains, begs off, or wants *something* in return. Yeah, you know. I'm pretty sure I'm not the only woman this happens to. Maybe that's why the salon I frequent is always full of women dozing through their pedicures. They're just blissed out beyond belief.

Some of my friends refuse pedicures because they can't stand having anyone touch their feet. They're just unbearably ticklish or squeamish or embarrassed at how their feet look—bunions or bad toenails or the like. Or, if diabetic, they need to be especially careful at avoiding infection. And, if one equates touch with physical abuse, there's every right to avoid anything that makes one feel vulnerable.

The crazy thing with touch is that you do become vulnerable. Another human being enters into your personal space. This can be unnerving.

There's another reason people don't want to be touched. It's because they have been so disappointed or humiliated by life that they emotionally wall themselves off as a protective device. If someone were to touch you with compassion and understanding, the wall might shatter like glass and you'd simply be a pile of broken shards.

This was my mother. A child of divorce in the 1920s, she was raised by Victorian grandparents in the Depression-era South. Mom grew up feeling old before her time, stigmatized and abandoned. She was only seventeen when she married my father in the summer of 1941. She expected him to be her knight in shining armor, a husband and a strong father figure who would provide the stability and home life she craved. Six months later, Pearl Harbor was attacked and Dad was shipped overseas. When he returned in 1945, he physically had survived the carnage of five major invasions but he was an emotional cripple. We call it post traumatic stress syndrome today (PTSD), and he suffered classic symptoms: night terrors, delusions, anxiety, survivor guilt, suicidal thoughts, and extreme fatigue. Mother recalled one night shortly after his return where Dad leaped out of bed in the middle of the night screaming that he was drowning in blood. He overturned every drawer in the house looking for ammunition, and threatened to kill my small brother, my mother, himself, or all three. Therapy? Forget it. He wouldn't talk about what happened to him during the war. Ever. Like so many veterans of that generation, he was expected to buck up, put up, and shut up.

Mother couldn't understand why Dad wasn't the same happy-go-lucky man she married before the war. Couldn't he just pick up where he left off? Her disappointments in him mounted. He held various jobs—at least two at a time, to be sure—but he wasn't rising up any corporate ladders without a college degree. School was never his thing, anyway. He preferred working with his hands. So money was always tight. He drank. A lot. His friends loved him, and he was the life of every party, but most considered him a sweet, sad clown. Mother despised him and blamed him for all her unfulfilled dreams. Bitterness ate away at her and her immune system crumped. She was always sick: lupus, rheumatoid arthritis, bursitis, gastrointestinal distress, and severe depression. She denied the depression, snapping, "I'm not depressed. I'm just angry at everyone!" Mom moved into the guestroom and told Dad if he ever touched her again, she'd file for divorce. So poor Dad stayed out of her way, taking refuge in his vegetable garden or in his basement workshop. If only it had been acceptable to talk about these things! But Depression-Era folks kept their mouths shut. Therapy was for crazy people. Talking just rehashes things you're trying hard to forget. None of that goddammed touchy-feely stuff for them.

Years later, this physical drought trickled down to me. One day when I was about fifteen, I hugged Mom and realized with a shock that she wasn't hugging me back. Her arms hung down stiffly at her sides, like downturned tree limbs, weeping under a heavy rain. It was as if she didn't remember how to respond anymore. Not even one of those pithy-patty side hugs that women are so good at when pretending to care.

Psychotherapist Katherine Schafler writes, "Another way to say that you are grieving is that part of you is stuck in a moment of time."[1] She asserts that one must touch one's loss, and with it all the anger, bitterness, and emotion that comes with it. Schafler says, "You have to pick it up (grief), hold it, feel the weight of it in your hands, on your heart, and within your life. You have to feel the whole loss. Grief demands to be felt with an insistence that needs no sleep. You either allow yourself to encounter the feelings or you remain encased in a shell of yourself under a misguided sense of self-protection."[2] We must force ourselves, then, to dig deeply into our souls and touch that which is the most painful if we are to begin to heal.

I am a blessed woman. Throughout my entire life, I've only experienced loving touch. I've never been a victim of violence or abuse. The closest I've come to understanding this unique type of hell is through my pastoral encounters with trauma patients.

On chaplaincy call at our county hospital one evening, I was paged to the Emergency Room. Things were busy, and the staff was rushing here and there, attending to those admitted. The charge

---

1. Schafler, "One Thing No One Ever Says," https://thriveglobal.com/stories/the-one-thing-no-one-ever-says-about-grieving/.

2. Schafler, "One Thing No One Ever Says," https://thriveglobal.com/stories/the-one-thing-no-one-ever-says-about-grieving/.

nurse directed me to a young woman who "needed counseling." Dutifully, I walked over to the patient, who was sitting impatiently on a gurney. I noticed a fresh cast on her right arm. She was in a hurry to leave and really didn't want to talk to me.

I was curious about her, though. She was only twenty-four and remarkably beautiful in spite of her torn shirt, bruised face and disheveled hair. What in the world had happened to her to make her dark eyes so empty?

"Hi, I'm the chaplain on duty tonight. Is there anything I can do to help you?" She stared at the ground. "No. I just want to go home." A few silent moments passed, and I gamely tried again. "I see you've got a cast. Did you have an accident?" She looked at me with pained impatience, indicating that I was, quite simply, a complete idiot. "Yeah. My boyfriend hit me and he broke my arm." Shocked, my mouth engaged, but not my brain. *Stupid brain!* "What! Why did he hit you?" "Because I needed to use his car to take our son to the doctor. He's sick." "But . . . but why?" I stammered. This was something my sheltered, white-bread self just couldn't comprehend. She sighed at my cluelessness. "Because he wanted to go party. He wouldn't let me use his car. I tried to open the car door and he beat me up. He's done it before. It's just how it is. Hey, can you get me out of here? I need to get back to my other kids." "Other kids?" *Shit!* "Yeah, I have four other little ones at home." "Are your kids in danger?" "Nah. He only hits me."

I took her left hand as gently as I knew how and said, "Can we talk to the Social Worker to see if we can get you a safe place to stay? Please?" She shook her head. "I live with my parents." *Jesus, the plot just kept thickening.* "Can't they protect you?" "Nah. They're afraid. They're old. They don't speak English. He threatens them. Look, I need to get home. My kids need me." I was too upset to speak. How could she accept this horrible Möbius loop of despair? She looked past me and her eyes grew very old. "If I try to leave, he'll hurt me worse. It's best if I just get out of here now."

How I wanted to hug her! To envelop her in an embrace that caused her to melt into a puddle of trust at my feet! But like my mother years before, this young woman might have shattered if

Palliare

I had dared to try and break through her protective walls. It was only bit of control she still had left. The social worker had quietly placed a call to CPS and APS, so there was little else I could do. I gave her a bus pass and watched her limp slowly out the sliding ER doors into the night.

The human body is a collection of organs functioning inside a big bag of skin, its largest organ. Scientists don't really know how many nerve endings are a part of our makeup, but it's a good guess to say that our bodies contain at least fifty trillion of them. Touch is part of our genetic make-up. Our need for touch helps to define us as human. A lack of touch results in what dome doctors are now calling "touch hunger." Hospital and nursing home patients are especially at risk. In my experience, a lack of loving touch can contribute to an increased risk of depression and a reduced will to live. As I am writing this book in the midst of the COVID pandemic, isolation and touch hunger are even more rampant because of contact precautions (contact isolation) and loved ones being prevented from visiting.

I used to dread chaplain assignments with "contact isolation" marked on the door. A patient identified as "contact isolation" suffers from a contagious disease or condition that requires everyone who enters to wear a hospital-issued plastic gown and gloves to prevent the spread of infection. Pre-COVID, a sign on the door indicated you had to wear a facemask unless you wanted to flirt with tuberculosis, viral meningitis, pneumonia or emphysema. Now masks are mandatory for everyone present. If you are sick enough to merit contact or airborne isolation, chances are you're in the ICU. And that's even more isolating. You might be hooked up to chest tubes, IV drips, oxygen masks, catheters, or a ventilator. I dreaded these visits, not because I didn't like the patients or families personally. That had nothing to do with it. What I hated was wearing the mask, gown, and gloves. They're bulky and hot, and worse, they restrict the skin-to-skin contact so important when comforting anxious patients. Wearing a mask obliterates your facial expression and makes you just one more cyborg in the alien space pod that is a typical American ICU.

All I Want is World Peace and a Pedicure

I especially hated visiting patients on ventilators because of the complete de-humanization it indicated. On a ventilator, the body cannot breathe on its own or talk, and cannot communicate except in rudimentary ways, provided the patient is conscious. Touch is plasticene. It's not easy to hold hands that are bruised and invaded by IVs, or pat skin that is breaking down. Yet that is when it is most important. Wearing plastic gloves is hospital policy, but to me, it was a hand condom that prevented the invasion of pulse and warmth. Sometimes (pre-COVID, mind you) I'd stealthily remove one glove so that I could gently stroke a hot forehead. I was determined to restore (if just for a moment) that person's dignity and sense of self. When I did try to feed a patient's touch hunger, it never failed to bring even the weakest smile of appreciation. An *agape* meal in miniscule bites, but a nourishing communion nonetheless.

Sometimes we simply don't have control over how we get touched, or when, or by whom. But sometimes we do. In the Gospel of Mark, the story is told of a woman who hemorrhaged for twelve years (Mark 5:25–34). Under the laws of the time, she could not leave her house. She couldn't shop, visit friends, or worship. No one was allowed to touch her. Friends and family she may have had gradually drifted away from her. She was alone in her suffering. So much loss! What grief she must have experienced! Like so many of us, life bled her dry. Where to even begin to put the pieces of her broken life back together?

She might have remained like this until she died if things had not changed. But things did change, for one day this woman decided that she needed to be touched by someone who cared. She had heard about a man named Jesus and how he had healed others. Something in her that day made her get up, get dressed, leave her house (perhaps for the first time in twelve years!) and take her fate into her own hands. Make no mistake. It was she who reached out and touched Jesus's cloak. She wanted his power, and he wanted to give it to her, and it became hers. Healing and peace came through a deliberate act of life-giving touch. Empowerment came from a place deep within her soul that had enough and screamed, "This is bullshit! No more!"

Palliare

It is hard to engage in honest dialogue with ourselves. It can hurt. Picking up our grief and holding it can hurt. And it's that fear of being hurt that cripples us. We struggle along, not even allowing God to dialogue with us, and in so doing, we deny God's desire to touch us down to the depths of our very souls with his love. Such divine touch involves us making a choice in which our vulnerability can become a renewed strength and a source of healing. Frederick W. Schmidt writes, "A passivity that takes refuge in a baptized fatalism or a caution that feeds spiritual inertia can represent a far larger defection from what we are called to do than any choice we might make."[3]

We are called to dig down into our guts, like a gardener raking mercilessly in the dirt, to root out the seeds that threaten to choke us off from living fully. We need to dig up our pain, struggling to get at the root of it, and making sure we get all of it. Then we must hold it, not fearing the dirt on ourselves. Finally, we must feel the weight of it before we can let it go. Only in touching our pain can we truly be free.

---

3 Schmidt, *What God Wants*, 88–90.

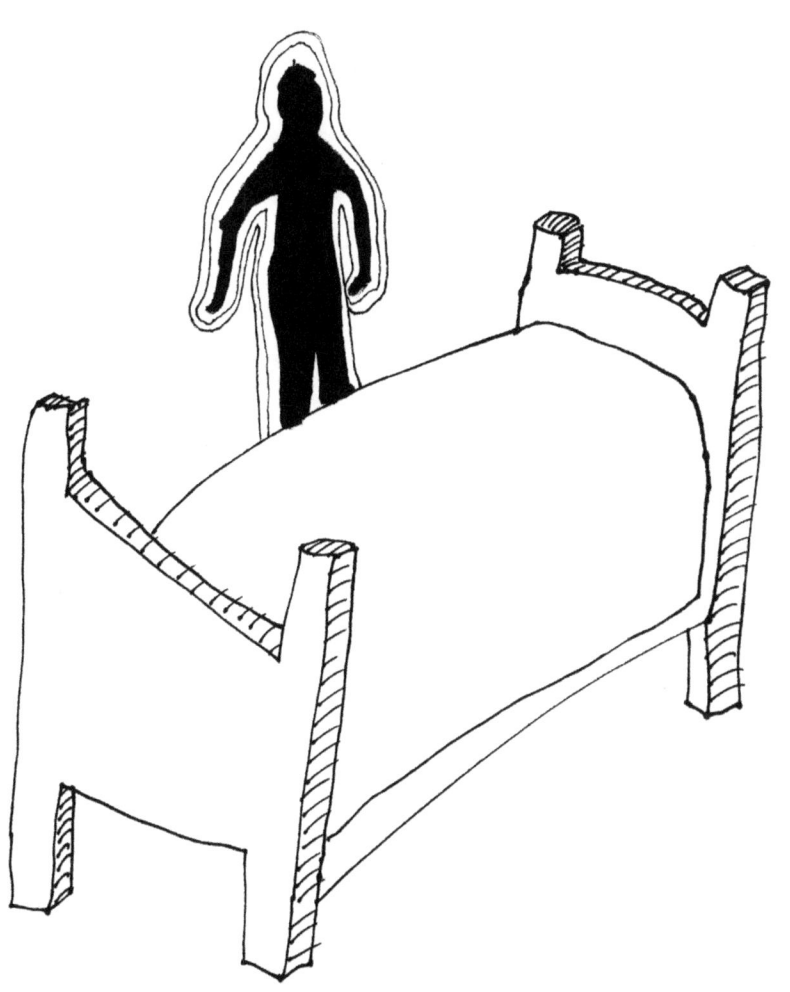

Glossary

1. Advanced Directives: directives to physicians that indicate a person's last medical treatment wishes, including orders requesting that artificial nutrition, hydration, or resuscitation be performed or withheld. Such directives usually include a next of kin designated to make decisions for the patient in case he or she is incapacitated. Advance Directive documents include the Do Not Resuscitate Order, the Out of Hospital Do Not Resuscitate Order, and the Directive to Physicians (sometimes known as a "Living Will.") These documents can vary from state to state.
2. Baptism: the rite of Christian initiation into the full Christian community, the church.
3. Bereavement: the psycho-social-emotional-spiritual experience of loss.
4. Grief: the psycho-social-emotional-spiritual responses to loss resulting in deep sadness, bewilderment, depression, anger, shock, bargaining, and ultimately acceptance of the loss.
5. Grief Support: that which assists persons suffering from grief and loss, including but not limited to classes, peer groups,

Glossary

books, videos, pamphlets, personal and group counseling, discussion groups, etc.

6. Hospice: an interdisciplinary approach to compassionate care and alleviation of suffering at the end of life that does not work in conjunction with life-sustaining treatment. May be offered in a hospital, hospice facility, or in-home setting.
7. Interdisciplinary: professional collaboration between persons of different medical specialties.
8. ICU: Intensive Care Unit.
9. Life-Sustaining Treatment: any medical measures implemented by physicians to keep a patient alive, including but not limited to artificial respiration, cardio-pulmonary resuscitation, mechanical ventilators, artificial nutrition and hydration, medications to stabilize blood pressure, etc.
10. NICU: Neo-Natal Intensive Care Unit.
11. Palliative Care: an interdisciplinary approach to compassionate care and alleviation of suffering at the end of life that may or may not work in conjunction with all life-sustaining treatment, usually within a hospital setting.
12. Resources: materials that aid and educate persons, such as tracts, flyers, letters, pamphlets, CDs, DVDs, books, newsletters, and electronic media.

Bibliography

Balk, David, et al. *Handbook of Thanatology*. Florence, KY: Routledge, 2007.
Dictionary.com. "Icon." http://dictionary.reference.com/browse/icon.
Episcopal Church. *The Book of Common Prayer*. New York: Church, 1979.
Fine, Robert L. "The Imperative for Hospital-Based Palliative Care: Patient, Institutional and Societal Benefits." Paper presented at the Office of Clinical Ethics, Baylor Health Care System, Dallas, TX, March 9, 2004.
―――. "Achieving Excellence in Palliative Care: Improving the Care of the Dying by Improving Care of the Living." Paper presented at the Palliative Care Training Seminar, Dallas, TX, January 23, 2009.
Hart, Thomas. *The Art of Christian Living*. New Jersey: Paulist, 1980.
Kubler-Ross, Elizabeth. *On Death and Dying*. New York: Macmillan, 1969.
McKnight, Scot. *A Community Called Atonement*. Nashville: Abingdon, 2007.
McTierman, John, dir. *Die Hard*. 1988; Los Angeles: Twentieth Century Fox.
Rando, Therese. *How To Go on Living When Someone You Love Dies*. Lexington, MA: Lexington, 1988.
Schafler, Katherine. *Thrive Global*. "The One Thing No One Ever Says about Grieving." https://thriveglobal.com/stories/the-one-thing-no-one-ever-says-about-grieving/.
Schmidt, Frederick W. *What God Wants for Your Life: Answers to Deepest Questions*. New York: HarperCollins, 2005.
Steinhauser, K. E., et al. "Factors Considered Important at the End of Life by Patients, Family, Physicians and Other Care Providers." *Journal of the American Medical Association* 284 (2000) 2476–82.
Tolstoy, Leo. *The Death of Ivan Ilyich*. New York: Tribeca, 2010.
Your Life Talks, "Dame Cicely Saunders—Pioneer of the Modern Hospice Movement," https://yourlifetalks.com/dame-cicely-saunders-pioneer-of-the-modern-hospice-movement/.

www.ingramcontent.com/pod-product-compliance
Lightning Source LLC
Chambersburg PA
CBHW071155090426
42736CB00012B/2341